Practicing the Presence of Peace

Bear Jack Gebhardt

natural
of this.

Thank you,
sister, for
being there,
here.

~Bear

December,
2009

PathBinder Publishing, LLC
www.PathBinder.com
www.HeatherHummel.net

Cover Design: Sam Gebhardt
www.SamGebhardt.com

*If we are peaceful, if we are happy, we can smile
and blossom like a flower, and everyone in our
family, our entire society, will benefit from our
peace.*

      -- Thich Nhat Hanh

 For Mahatma Gandhi, Muhammad Ali, Thich
Nhat Hanh, Badshaw Khan, William Sloane
Coffin Jr., Bishop Desmond Tutu, George Fox,
and the Brothers Berrigan, all of whom taught
peace and lived peace in the midst of turmoil, and
for Mike Farrell, who with great bravery has taken
up the ancient mantel, and finally, for Brother
Lawrence, without whom this work would not be.

*** *Acknowledgements* ***

Once again, thanks go to "Dr. Happiness," Christian Almayrac, M.D., for making it all so plain.

And I especially want to thank Heather Hummel, editor and publisher of PathBinder Publishing. Heather is so in tune with her own joy and peace that when she spotted this little castaway puppy lying hidden by the side of the road, she reached out, picked it up, brought it home and nurtured it, softly, tenderly, patiently, into the happy healthy romper that it is today. Thank you, again, Heather.

TABLE OF CONTENTS

Editor's Introduction: Who Was Dr. Charlie?

Charles Bernard Lawrence, Ph.D., ("Dr. Charlie,") passed away in late 2007, at aged 94, with a spontaneous grin on his face. We miss his physical presence deeply. His grin, thank God, stays with us.

His spontaneous grin had been with him, on and off, but mostly on, almost all day every day for the final 76 of his 94 years. This small book contains fifteen of his letters and the record of four of his conversations, all regarding his daily discipline of the practice of peace — the discipline that elicited his grin. This book shares Dr. Charlie's grin and the practice behind it with the wider world.

In his personal life, Dr. Charlie was a family man, with three children, eight grandchildren, two great-grandchildren, and a wife of 62 years, who had preceded him in death by a decade. In his professional life, he was a small town psychologist, what he himself referred to as "an anonymous nurturer of humanity's peace." The power and beauty of his simple personal and professional life is now available to a wider audience through the conversations and letters contained in this small volume. As far as we know, this is the only written record of and instruction of Dr. Charlie's simple and profound discipline of peace, which is also the discipline of joy.

We all know what it means to be happy, to be at peace, but for most of us, our experience of peace is fleeting, quick, here then gone. One minute we're at peace, then for the next week or so we're not. And yet, according to the greatest thinkers as far back as Aristotle and as recent as Deepok Chopra, Wayne Dwyer or Andrew Weil, "...*the most practical thing we can do in our lives, for our health, for our bank account, for our vocation, for our very salvation, is to be happy, and live in peace.*" When we say it out loud, as simple as this, few would argue. Clearly, living in peace and being happy is the most practical and thus the most powerful thing we can do with our lives, not only for ourselves but also for those around us.

"No, no," some would argue. "To love God with all our heart and soul and mind and to love our neighbor as ourselves," *these* are the most important things. (*Upon these two commandments*, Jesus said, *hang all the law and prophets*.)

Of course that's true. But Dr. Charlie would suggest that if we aren't *at peace* with God's creation, if we aren't *at peace* with the day He has brought, the work, the traffic, the crabgrass, if we aren't *at peace* with the people He (She) has put before us, if we aren't *at peace* with this daily round of affairs we are in, and the people we are in it with, how can we possibly be loving the Creator? Dr. Charlie suggests that being at peace is the one true dependable sign that we are in fact knowing and loving God and loving our neighbor. Peace, love and joy, Dr. Charlie said, are three different words pointing to the exact same wordless Presence.

So if living our daily lives in peace is indeed so important why do we, at least sometimes, let many hours, or many

2

days, even weeks (or months or decades) pass without our conscious, deliberate remembrance of peace? Why do we forget to practice something so important as our own peace?

It's because our culture teaches us that peace will be the *result* of something we do, will be *caused* by something external. So we work for results, work for causes, and hope that peace will be the result of our efforts. We are falsely taught that we must work for peace, or let it come upon us unexpectedly in some rare occasions. We are taught that peace is something outside that we must go get, or stumble upon, or await its arrival. So we work and wait for it to happen, try to make it happen, and when desperate enough, scramble for its crumbs.

Dr. Charlie encouraged a different view. "As human beings we are all already peaceable," he says. "Peace is the first quality of consciousness itself. So we never have to *do* anything, *be* anything, *go* anywhere, *be* anywhere, *have* something, or even get rid of something before we are allowed to access our own easy, natural peace. We can access peace whenever and wherever we choose, regardless of the results or lack of results from our efforts in the outer world. I've proven the practice of peace in my own life. And I've helped my family and friends and clients to also prove that peace is possible, is natural, in spite of what is happening in the outer world. Sticking with our own natural peace is very practical, and it is what most helps and heals the outer world."

For Dr. Charlie, practicing his natural peace was the same thing as practicing love, or compassion, forgiveness, friendship, happiness. He assured us that we don't have to wait for outer conditions to be "right" before we experience love, friendship, happiness or peace. The time and place for peace is always "right now, right here."

3

Practicing the Presence of Peace

Dr. Charlie was not an ambitious man, in terms of gaining personal fame, professional stature or financial rewards, although all of these did in fact come to him in some measure as a by-product of his peaceable daily disciplines. Dr. Charlie's ambition was consistently focused on increasing one skill: being able to move in peace through the circumstances of his life, both inner and outer, and thus living in peace with all those with whom he shared his daily circumstances (again, inwardly and outwardly!).

Dr. Charlie's work with his clients was, on the surface, quite uncomplicated. He taught all of us a simple way to access our own peace, and he showed us why we could — and should — give priority to this practice of peace above all other things in our lives. He seemed uninterested in establishing any particular school of psychology or therapy based on his work, or initiating any movement or in making a name for himself. Rather, he was interested solely in helping his friends and clients to experience and magnify the peace in our lives. This, he said, was a sufficiently cosmic challenge to keep him occupied for a lifetime.

Dr. Charlie practiced his peaceable disciplines with as much depth while cleaning his garage or doing his laundry as he did while counseling clients or giving seminars. He wrote, "I consider myself just as much at work while riding the city bus or shopping for groceries as when I have a client behind closed doors. Peace is the treasure to be discovered in every circumstance."

He confessed, "I have trained myself to simply, consistently entertain only those thoughts and stories with which I am at peace. And I have trained myself to be at peace with thoughts and stories with which I previously might not have been at peace. One has to be brave, and somewhat of a loner, to take up this training. But I am now so habituated to abiding with peace that I am seldom ever without it. The practice of peace is now as common, ordinary

4

and fixed in my life as is tying my shoes and brushing my teeth."

As will be discovered in the pages ahead, Dr. Charlie considers peace to be the most moral of all *asanas*, or positions one might assume in one's life.

As far as his religious affiliations, Dr. Charlie was a bit on the fringe. He sometimes attended Unity Church, or the Quaker (Friends) Meeting, the Mennonite Assembly or the Christian Science Church or the Church of Religious Science, though he often accepted invitations from clients and friends to attend and even speak at more mainstream communities. He enjoyed the rousing music and multi-media presentations at the Timberline Free Evangelical Church in our town, and enjoyed retreats at the Shambhala Center and Thursday evening Theravada Buddhist Meditations. He was a frequent visitor and "guest communicator" at Heart Mountain Monastery, an informal Taoist Christian community. (In this capacity he considered himself to be only a "lay monk" whose primary association with the community was simply an inner agreement to live in peace and happiness.) He would, when appropriate, suggest to one or another of his clients that they might find one or another particular church or discipline or retreat to be beneficial, or that they might want to take up one or another prayer or meditation discipline. All such recommendations and suggestions were spontaneous and free of bias for or against such participation. He was not a "recruiter" for any particular faith or formula. He was simply a peaceful man, sharing his discoveries.

Dr. Charlie passed over to Spirit at age 94, in his sleep, at home in his own bed. On the day of his passing he had taken his customary three-mile walk around the city park lake, feeding breadcrumbs to the ducks and geese. He had kept two professional appointments that day, seeing one old client and one new client, a neighbor's niece who was just passing through town. He had cooked his own supper of rice and vegetables that he customarily took with a small glass of red wine. That evening he called two of his three children, "checking in," as was his habit several times a week. That day, he had run a load of washing—his "whites": t-shirts, socks and underwear. (So he died with clean underwear!)

It has been my honor to collect and edit this little record of Dr. Charlie's mind and heart. Before his passing, Dr. Charlie and I had been friends for over thirty years. (I still consider him one of my best friends, though now our friendship unfolds on a subtler plane!) I was also once a "patient" of Dr. Charlie, (though Dr. Charlie never called us "patients") and a fellow monk, fellow grandpa and African Violet enthusiast.

The first part of this book consists of the notes I made from four of the many conversations I had with Dr. Charlie early in our relationship. (I was more prone to keeping such notes back then.) I first went to Dr. Charlie on the recommendation of one of my university professors when I was engaged in graduate studies. I was suffering from a recent romantic break-up, was impoverished, ill, and probably near a nervous breakdown. I was also still totally uncertain of my life's direction (or purpose!). In our first meetings together Dr. Charlie gave me what he called "a simple tune-up" (but what I experienced as major overhaul!), and then he gave me the tools to do my own tune-ups. Looking back, I realize I've been pretty much humming along ever since. (Thanks again, Dr. Charlie!) Most of his "patients" have had the same simple, yet profoundly life-changing experience.

The second part of this book consists of fifteen letters (appearing here lightly edited) which Dr. Charlie wrote to several of his colleagues, associates and "client friends" who had asked him directly or indirectly to please give them something in writing regarding what they had learned and experienced in his company.

As the reader will soon see, Dr. Charlie did not hesitate to speak of God, or of Christ, of the Divine Presence or the Buddha Mind because he recognized that these words reflected the deeper concerns and understandings of the cultural traditions of many of those who came to him. Dr. Charlie himself came out of the western Jewish-Christian tradition (with a Ph.D. from Kansas State) and yet his work as presented in this book does not require acceptance, or adherence or "belief" in any particular or general spiritual or psychoanalytical system. "Peace is the meat," he says. "After you know peace, all else is gravy."

The "meat" which Dr. Charlie brought to the earth continues to nourish hungry people (even vegetarians!) long after he has gone. Dr. Charlie's "meat" appears not only in this volume, but also in the lives of all of us with whom he shared his simple methods. Our own lives feel (and feed!) the continuing reverberations of his beautiful life-long love affair with peace.

From Dr. Charlie we learned that it is possible to awaken each morning happy and at peace with the day ahead, and to proceed from that first moment in our small affairs and large with a clear awareness of the immanence of Peace.[1]* From him we learned that it is in fact possible (and advisable!) to move through all our relationships, fulfill all our responsibilities, journey through all our urban and suburban

---

[1]The word Peace is often (though not always or consistently) capitalized throughout this book, in keeping with Dr. Charlie's own practice, as an indication of the Divine nature of peace, similar to the word God or Christ or Buddha or Love, Joy, or Happiness—all, in context, qualities, or characteristics of the Divine. More about this will be found in the pages that follow.

adventures with a conscious devotion to, and awareness of the immutable, transcendent peaceable Presence. He demonstrated that we could go to bed at night having gone through our entire day simply "at peace." And that we can dream pleasant dreams and awaken the next morning to begin the process all over again. Dr. Charlie proved that peace is in fact the natural and spontaneous state of every human being, and thus it is the most moral way of living. He proved that peace, when repeatedly accessed, imbues a life with grace, power and beauty.

"Peace is the meat;" he said, "after you know peace, all else is gravy." This book presents numerous meals that, it is hoped, every reader will find easily eaten and deeply nourishing. *Bon Appetit!*

Bear Jack Gebhardt, Senior Librarian
Heart Mountain Monastery

First Conversation:
Peace Is the Background of All That Is

I first met Dr. Charlie on the 3rd of August, 1976. As already mentioned, (see Editor's Introduction) because of various mental and emotional problems I had been experiencing, I had been referred to him by one of my university professors. When we first met, Dr. Charlie was in his early 60's, silver haired, tall, thin, and beaming. He had an office attached to the back of his home in the old part of town. After visiting briefly at his front door, we walked through his tidy home out the back to a small screened-in porch attached to his office. We looked out onto a flower garden. He poured lemonade. Sitting and talking with him was like sitting and talking with a friendly neighbor.

In our first meeting, after we briefly discussed why I was there, he told me that for some unexplained reason he'd had been blessed with a life-changing experience when he was only 18 years-old, and that since that day peace had never left him. Peace was his life's

9

companion. He said this very simply, just stating the facts, without pride or embellishment or expecting anything from me. It was as if he was telling me the names of the flowers there in front of us. This ongoing awareness of peace, he said, was the most important thing in his life, and in his work, and that peace is what he had to teach, and share, and show me how to access.

Obviously, I was quite willing to learn what he had to teach about peace—my life was in great turmoil. First, though, I was curious about what had happened to him. He told me the story.

When he was 18 he had been at a park in the city in early spring, sitting on a bench, waiting for a friend, idly aware of a group of young girls playing on the grass nearby. As he remembered it, the young girls were all wearing bright colored dresses, coats and caps. Then he noticed a bent old woman, using a cane, wearing a dark overcoat and scarf, making her way out from the surrounding evergreen trees. Her path took her through the middle of the young girls. At one point, the old woman stopped and looked at the young girls and smiled, and one of the young girls ceased playing for a moment, smiled back and waved lightly at the old woman, before resuming her play. Observing the simple interaction had likewise brought a smile to Charlie.

"Suddenly, I saw it was the same smile," Dr. Charlie said, "arising from the same background peace, in the young girl and in the old woman and in me. In that moment I felt the presence, the background peace in my own heart. At that moment I realized that peace, or joy, or happiness—these are words for the same impersonal presence—was absolutely everywhere. It is this peace that animates everything and everyone. This impersonal yet personal peace was absolutely still, yet it was alive, powerful. It was this peace—God's Peace, or life's peace, if you want to call it that, but peace, nevertheless—that was behind the winter and spring, summer and autumn, old age and youth, even though peace itself never aged, never went anywhere."

As we sat on his back porch, Dr. Charlie himself was beaming, animated, yet obviously at peace, just telling the story that I'm sure he must have told a thousand times.

"*God's* peace?" I asked. I was going through my agnostic/atheistic/existentialist period.

"You don't have to call it God's peace, if you don't want." Dr. Charlie laughed. "I just *saw* peace. I saw life itself. The words to describe it don't matter. I suddenly was aware of the impersonal peace behind it all, in it all; behind and in the words, and forms and time and space. I was simply aware of the background peace, everywhere. I saw that everything always comes out of and then fades back into the background!"

"Okay," I said. He wasn't trying to make a case. He was just telling me what happened.

"In that moment," he went on, "I realized that peace itself isn't personal. Or it isn't just personal. And peace isn't just the absence of conflict, or turmoil. Peace is a power and intelligence in itself, a presence in itself. .

"There in the park I saw the light of this presence everywhere, not only in the young girls but also in the grass that they were playing on and in the tall

11

evergreens that surrounded them, the blue sky in the background. I could see that the background peace was present in that moment in that old woman's smile but that it had also been present throughout all the moments of her life's history, whether she knew it or not. I could also see that the presence of peace there in that moment where all these young girls were playing—this same peace would also be there in all of their future moments, again, whether they recognized this presence or not. I was completely engulfed. I could *see* that life's peace was present everywhere, within and without. I saw that peace was the nature—the essence, the intelligent power—of life itself. So peace was in the distant traffic, the horns honking, the buildings, the birds flying above us and in the sky through which the birds were flying. I saw that peace was in me, and I was in it. It was me. I was it... "

He smiled, closed his eyes for a brief moment. It was quiet. Then he opened his eyes and looked at me and spoke very softly, but plainly. "I sensed in that moment," he said, "how it is that peace and the Spirit of God and the nature of life are all the same, all one presence, regardless of the words used to describe them. You can call it the Buddha mind, or the Tao, or the Atman, or Brahman, Allah, Amma, Da, the evolutionary impulse. It makes no difference what words you use. A wordless, intelligent presence is there behind the words. And that presence is peaceable. That presence is peace itself! "

In that moment he grinned real big at me. I just nodded. It was as if I could see the wordless, joyful peace—life's peace—coming out through his eyes. His grinning was contagious. I intuited in that moment that what he was talking about – the background peace, the wordless peace – was real, alive and present, and that I might be able to know it, see it, just as he had. Looking back on my life, I see that it was in this moment that I started to wake up.

He went on to say that this awareness-- or at least the understanding – of the infinite and immediate nature of peace has been with him ever since that moment in the park. He said that at that moment he was set free of the false belief that peace was the *result* of something or someone, or simply the absence of conflict or turmoil. "Peace is always present," he said. Peace was not ever arbitrary or narrow or the result of some particular person's special skill or luck or possession or relationship or circumstance. "Peace can be experienced personally but it's not personal," he said. "That's my personal experience." And he laughed again.

Dr. Charlie said he didn't know why he had been given at such a young age this vision – this simple awareness – of the breadth and depth and immediacy of impersonal peace. He confessed that, although his ability to more consistently access and enjoy this impersonal peace had steadily improved, this first *vision* of the absolute nature of impersonal peace had not expanded or contracted in the almost 50 years since that moment in time.

Shortly after this revelation in the park Dr. Charlie went to work on a trash truck. He said he would have been content to spend his life picking up trash, as he was completely happy, at peace, un-ambitious, not worried about his future. "It was as if I had won the lotto," he said. "I was at peace, and thus happy, every day. What more did I need or expect from life?"

Nevertheless, after several years working on the trash truck Dr. Charlie was moved to enroll at the university. An urge had risen up in him to become a psychologist so he could help people who were unnecessarily unhappy. He also theorized that perhaps by working with the sorrows and turmoil's and illnesses of others he would bring his seemingly undiminishable ability to be at peace into line with more traditional natures. "I thought I might be a little crazy," he laughed, "being so happy and peaceful every day, there on the trash truck. I was at peace with my happiness, but it did seem unusual."

At the university, he discovered his experience of peace remained present, buoyant and full throughout both his undergraduate and graduate studies. His experience of peace became even more magnified as he began sharing his peace and his methods for accessing peace with others in his private practice.

"I've learned that living in peace is the most practical and most natural and most generous thing we can do for ourselves and for everybody around us," he said. "I'm convinced that some day everybody will come to understand and practice this simple truth."

"How can we?" I asked. "Wouldn't we all have to have the same kind of mystical experience that you did there in the park?"

"No, not at all," he said, excitedly. "I don't know why that experience happened to me. But I have learned since then that anybody can access peace, whenever they choose. Do you want to know how?"

He grinned at me, waiting.

"Of course, yes," I said.

Again he laughed. "You practice peace simply by being at peace with the thoughts you are thinking," he said. "Being at peace with the stories you tell yourself. That sounds very simple. But that's all it takes."

"Sounds almost too easy," I said.

"*Almost* too easy," he said. "Easy to say, easy to learn. Not so easy, when first starting out, to practice."

"Be at peace with the thoughts we're thinking?" I repeated. "How?"

He grinned, and his eyes brightened (they were pretty bright to begin with.) He didn't respond right away, but instead held up one finger.

"That," he finally said. "May be the second most important question in the world."

"What? I asked.

"*How can we be at peace with our thoughts?* That's a very powerful question. One of the most powerful ever asked by any human being. Congratulations! If you can answer that question, you have the secret of life."

"So how can we be at peace with our thoughts?" I asked.

"Just ask," he said.

"Ask who?" I interrupted.

"Ask yourself. *Am I at peace with this thought, yes or no?* That's the first step in learning to be at peace with your thoughts. And it's the number one most important question we can ask. Simply ask, *"Am I at peace with this thought, yes or no?"*

"So then what?" I asked.

"If you are at peace with your thoughts, that's perfect. Keep thinking them. If you are at peace with what you are thinking, you don't need to do anything. Your life is already on track. If you aren't at peace with your thoughts, however, then you have two choices. Either drop those thoughts, those stories with which you are not at peace and find thoughts and stories with which you are more at peace, or keep thinking what you're thinking, but choose to *be at peace* with what a moment before you weren't at peace."

I nodded my head, but wasn't real sure I understood. He said it again, in a slightly different way.

"If you are at peace with your thoughts," he said, "you don't need to do anything. Being at peace with your thoughts is how you bring peace into your life. Be at peace with your thoughts, enjoy your thoughts, and the stories these thoughts are telling. The thoughts and stories with which you are at peace are your friends. Let them come and go freely. Let them introduce you to more peaceable thoughts and stories. You can trust thoughts and stories that you enjoy, with which you are peace.

"But if you aren't at peace with your thoughts—just like friends you aren't at peace with—you certainly don't want to spend much time with them, or follow them down to the cellar, see where they're going. They will only lead you to more thoughts you aren't at peace with, more dark stories. So if you aren't at peace with a thought, or a story, let it go, discard it and then find or create a thought or story that you find more peaceable. That's one option.

"The other option is if at first you aren't at peace with a thought or story then simply change your mind about it. Decide to make it your friend. You do this simply by choosing to *be at peace with the exact same thought* or story which a moment before you were not at peace.

"For example," he said. "Let's say you're working and your boss comes up and says, 'you're fired.' Would you be at peace with that thought? Would it be your friend?"

"No, probably not," I said.

"Probably not. But in the next moment, you are free to *choose* to be at peace with that thought, to be friendly toward it. You could even be happy with that thought! That's option b."

I laughed.

"You can choose to be at peace with almost any thought in the universe," he said. "Though we are not usually taught that we are this free."

I didn't know what to think. In fact, it seemed I wasn't thinking much at all. And I was quite peaceful about not thinking.

He said that if I practiced this way of thinking — practiced choosing thoughts and stories with which I was at peace — I would soon discover that my life was effortlessly filled with peace, and from there with power and beauty.

"It's actually that simple," he said, looking at me a bit sheepishly. He grinned, shrugged his shoulders. "I don't know why we aren't taught this simple thinking process in grade school."

I didn't know what to say. It made sense — simply entertain the thoughts and stories with which I was peace, and drop the ones I wasn't at peace with. Yet, again, it seemed almost *too* simple. And too dangerous. It seemed naïve. I was a graduate student, after all. I was very practiced at making life very complicated.

"So how do I know whether I'm at really peace with a thought or story, or am just avoiding an issue, or being foolish or naive?" I asked.

"Oh, that. That's easy," he said. "Again, you ask the question, 'Am I at peace with this thought, yes or no?' If the answer is not an immediate and spontaneous yes, it's a no." He grinned.

"If the answer isn't an immediate and spontaneous yes, it's a no," I repeated.

"That's it," he said. "It's black or white, yay or nay. Our peace is much too important to be fuzzy or unclear about whether we are with peace or not. So when you ask the question, if the answer as to whether you are at peace with a thought or story isn't an immediate and spontaneous yes, then it's a no."

"What about truth?" I asked. "Some thoughts or stories are true, but they aren't very peaceful. And some thoughts may be peaceful, but not true."

"First, I like to be linguistically precise," he laughed. "Thoughts themselves are neither peaceful nor un-peaceful. Nor are the stories we tell ourselves. You are either at peace with a thought or a story, or you aren't. The thought or story itself is neither peaceful nor un-peaceful. A thought with which you, personally, are at peace, I might not find peaceful. Or a thought I'm at peace with, you might not be. And a story I'm not at peace with today, I might be at peace with tomorrow. Or visa versa. Thoughts and stories themselves are neither peaceful nor un-peaceful." He had said it three times, very quick.

"Give me an example," I asked.

He laughed. "Okay. You might be at peace with the thought of drinking a 12 pack of beer, getting naked and riding your motorcycle a hundred miles an hour across the prairie." I laughed. "You might be at peace with that thought, that story, but I suspect your mother would not," he continued.

"I suspect you're right."

"And then let's say you actually do it," he said. "And then get arrested and thrown in the pokey."

"The pokey?"

"In jail. Sitting in jail, naked under a blanket, you might not be at peace with the naked motorcycle ride thought so much. Though no thought is forbidden. You can still be at peace with it if you choose."

"Okay, I see what you mean."

"The thought you are at peace with today, you might not be at peace with tomorrow. Or visa versa."

"Okay, yes. I follow you."

"So thoughts themselves are neither peaceful nor un-peaceful," he repeated. He was drilling it into my head. "We are either at peace with them or not. It's a subtle little point, but very powerful. It sets us free. Yes?"

"Yes, okay," I said again. Curiously, in that moment, my thoughts seemed quite peaceful.

19

Dr. Charlie went on to say that in his personal experience truth—the deepest truth, the lasting truth—*always* came out of peace, and was always joyous. He said that by using peace as a beacon by which to choose his thoughts he had discovered the deeper truths about life. "This is not what they teach in the universities," he laughed. "But it is what I teach." He let his voice drop, and then almost whispered. He encouraged me to not worry too much about whether a thought I was thinking was true. It was more important whether or not I was peace.. "This is a very blasphemous, and revolutionary way of thinking," he laughed.

"But just being aware that you are not at peace with a thought does not help you," he said. "The discipline only begins, only has benefit, when you actually *do* something about not being at peace with your thoughts. When you become aware that you are not at peace with a thought, you basically have two choices: either

    a.) Drop the thought you are not at peace with and choose or create a thought with which you are more at peace; or

    b.) Choose to be at peace with that thought which a moment before you were not at peace."

This was the third time he had repeated this simple practice. He pointed out, again, that with the first option, my thought changes. With the second option, my thought doesn't change but my attitude about it does.

"You are not obliged to think a particular thought just because it appears to be true," he said. "Or because others have put forth this thought as true, perhaps for many generations. Nor are you obliged to discard a thought just because it appears to be false, and everybody around you agrees that it is false. What appears to be true and what appears to be false always changes over time, both personally and culturally. What does not change is peace itself. As you allow your peace to be the only arbiter of your thoughts — regardless of appearances or cultural tradition — your very life becomes more true, more real, more grounded. Choose thoughts with which you are at peace. Abandon or realign yourself with the thoughts with which you aren't at peace. Being at peace with your thoughts is the absolute key. It leads to full, honest and successful living."

I had my doubts. We talked a bit more. I said I wasn't sure I was philosophically inclined to such "positive thinking." It seemed a bit unreal. Dr. Charlie laughed, and assured me that he was not simply suggesting "positive thinking." He said that he had observed that one could be at peace with any thought — positive or negative — at one moment or another, in one condition or another. He said that the wondrous results that had been brought about by people who practiced positive thinking were brought about *not* because the thoughts themselves were positive but rather because the people *were at peace with the thought, and thus enjoyed to think the thought!* He had also observed that the failures that had been experienced in positive thinking had likewise occurred not because the person's practice was insufficient but rather because of the person's *lack of peace* in the practice of thinking, a lack of peace in holding the thought!

He told me that my peace was the key for obtaining results with my thinking. He said again that peace is not a haphazard or occasional or a sporadic uprising, depending solely on the fortunate or misfortunate events of my life, but is rather a constant background presence, an unvarying option which I might profitably train myself to access.

"A peaceful state of mind," he said, "is what gives power to any discipline, be that discipline secular or spiritual." He said that the background peace contains within itself sufficient wisdom, intelligence, rhythm, pace, intensity, moderation and motive to guide each of us in anything we do, large or small. Whatever other discipline we take up, he said, peace should be our first discipline, because it's the master discipline.

I told him again that I was a bit shy, indeed skeptical of religious interpretations of the world. He said he often shared my skepticism and that his own experience had led him to conclude that we are safe when we focus on peace, as it reveals itself in our thinking. Doing this, he said, we will soon discover we are in flow with life itself. He said we don't need to believe one way or another — that this peace practice was a practical approach to managing our inner territory. Doing this, he said, we would soon discover that we were in constant communion with and service to what others might call God, or the Buddha Mind, or the Atman, or the quantum mechanics of life itself. But we didn't need such words or belief systems. He said that in his own understanding, peace itself is the sign and signature of the Divine Presence. However, someone else could be a complete atheist but if they were living a consciously peaceful life, they would spontaneously fulfill all the commandments of all the spiritual traditions.

In Dr. Charlie's presence, with his words, I found both my angst and my agnosticism starting to melt. Dr. Charlie continued, saying that his studies had led him to perceive that all of the horrors that had been committed down through history and justified under the guise of serving God all happened precisely because people were not at peace with themselves, not at peace in their lives. The peaceable, loving quality of the Divine had not been given its rightful, momentary authority. He said that he intuited that no man, when aware of either the natural background peace or the peace residing in his deepest heart, could ever truly be at peace persecuting, oppressing, cheating, punishing or killing another human being. He said that by focusing on accessing peace, as a personal discipline, that the necessity, willingness and opportunity to commit horrors against others always dissolves.

He pointed out the fact that most children around the world, most of the time, are already living in peace, and joy, even without a conscious understanding of these methods. He took this generally peaceable and happy conduct by most children, most of the time, as indicative of our natural inclinations and character. That we all—individually and collectively—have been so quick to abandon this naturally peaceful, joyful, loving character and go off in anger to war, large or small, has come about not because of our natural inclinations but rather because of faulty training and erroneous beliefs. He said he was quite hopeful—even with the horrors of war appearing nightly on our televisions—that the old faulty training and erroneous belief systems are now rapidly revealing themselves as inadequate and barbarous. He said he was confident that these old systems would soon dissolve in the true light—in the innate peace that the human population was now learning to honor and access. He said that he recognized that his own most important contribution to the world, to the ending of wars and the dissolution of erroneous beliefs and faulty training was for he himself to remain ever cognizant and responsive to the presence of peace, which is also the presence of happiness, in himself and others, within and without, near and far. His second most important contribution was to teach this simple method to others.

He said I myself could bring an end to the wars, my own wars and the wars of others, by patient and careful attention to the thoughts which I was holding, and the stories I was telling, be those thoughts and stories about small daily matters or universally profound topics. He said that my thoughts and stories either acted to magnify the background peace that is here, in which we all live, or the thoughts and stories I told myself were acting as clouds in front of that same peace. He assured me that peace would remain my essential nature regardless of whether I was magnifying the peace or covering it up with my thoughts. Peace was my nature whether I allowed it to show through or whether I covered it up.

We were coming to the end of our session.

"So," he said, "your homework, if you choose to do it, is to simply ask, *Am I at peace with this thought, yes or no.* If it's not an immediate and spontaneous yes, it's a no."

"Okay," I said, still a bit skeptical, but willing to try.

"But you can't stop there. If the answer is yes, you are peace with your thoughts, perfect. You're at peace with yourself and the world. But if the answer is no, you are not at peace, then you either drop the thought with which you are not at peace and find or create a thought with which you are more at peace, or..."

"Or I choose to be at peace with the thought which a moment before I was not at peace, like 'you're fired,'" I interrupted. He laughed. He had repeated the process so many times in that first session that I had it.

He said that if I was interested in further exploring the adventure and discipline of this peace practice, and working with him to magnify the peace in our own lives and in the world, he would be honored to work with me. He said that our work together would be not only to diminish my own personal distress but also to diminish and eventually overrule distress wherever we might encounter it. Our work together would be to undo the faulty training and belief systems of the whole world, starting with those faulty beliefs showing up in our own thought stream. If this was my desire, he said, he would welcome our association and would encourage me to come see him as often as I chose.

He cautioned me, though, that since this practice of peace was his only devotion and passion and love—his absolute way of life—that if I was not primarily interested in practicing "the art and science of peace," that his assistance in any other matter would probably be less than efficient, and our work together probably prove to be unprofitable. He grinned. "So do you want to continue to explore this practice of peace with me?"

I laughed. He already knew the answer. It was easy. "Sure," I said. "I'd be happy to!"

Our lemonade was finished. We stood, and he walked me down the walk to the front of the house, as we figured out when we would meet again. We shook hands, and then he laughed and gave me a quick hug. "I'm so happy to meet you," he said. "I look forward to working with you." And I could tell, it was true.

This was the end our first conversation, and the beginning of what turned out to be a 30-year friendship and adventure in practicing peace. This first meeting was the first of many, many wondrous blossomings that Dr. Charlie nourished in my life.

The Second Conversation:
Grin While You Pray

We had our second conversation ten days after our first, on another pleasant summer afternoon. Again we sipped lemonade as we sat on the screened-in porch at the back of his home. This time I had brought along a tape recorder, and asked if it would be okay to tape our session. He said he generally discouraged taping sessions or even taking notes, and instead encouraged his clients to simply be present, to enjoy the relationship and whatever unfolded, without thought for what it might bring or how it might later be used. I argued. I told him that as a graduate student I was so accustomed to taking notes and "getting it all down" for later that I was certain I would not be able to enjoy our conversations without some kind of record.

He laughed, and agreed to my taping. It's because of this that I have this somewhat lengthy, detailed account here, thirty years later, of our conversation. Hence, this is also the longest piece in the book. In later sessions I did take notes, but did not tape them, because he did show me how the quality of my listening was different when I was taping. The reader is, of course, not obliged to read this second conversation all the way through in a single sitting. Read until full, and then return when hungry.

This account may also seem somewhat repetitive, which in a way it is. And yet it was Dr. Charlie's returning to the same principles again and again from different directions, especially here in this second conversation, which allowed me to finally begin to release my habitual ways of relating to my thought stream in order to take up this new peace practice. I trust the reader will likewise be so motivated.

Dr. Charlie asked right off about my practice. I told him I'd been trying to engage the discipline — thinking thoughts with which I was at peace, dropping thoughts with which I was not at peace — but that I'd found it very difficult. I confessed that I had days go by without even thinking about it.

He assured me this was normal, but that I would discover my ability to stay in peace steadily growing over the following weeks and months. "It's like learning to play the piano," he said. "At first you play simple little tunes, and make little harmonies with chords, and you can enjoy this new talent, even just a few minutes every couple of days. As you continue to practice, your skills increase, and the pleasure you derive from the practice also increases, so you spend more time with it. Your peace is like the piano. All the keys and the potential for wondrous music are already there inside you. You are just now learning to play, to bring out new harmonies."

With his words, or maybe it was just his company, I started to relax, and felt relieved about my seeming inability to stay in my peace, and my inattention to the work itself.

"I've been at it a long time," he said. "I've trained myself to let peace guide me everywhere, always. You can train yourself in this way, too. When you directly observe that honoring your peace, experiencing your peace, truly is the most practical thing you can do, both for yourself and for everybody around you, then the discipline quickens, takes on a delightful urgency."

He suggested that although the basic work was always a matter of paying attention to what we were thinking, and more specifically paying attention to whether we *were at peace* with what we were thinking, that in the beginning of our practice we could also ask whether we were at peace with what we were doing or saying.

"In my own life, if I am not at peace with what I'm doing, I either stop doing it or choose to be at peace with it," he said. "If I am not at peace with what I'm saying, I immediately stop saying it. Staying with my peace is that important to me. I've found I can trust my sense of peace to guide me in everything I say and do and think. "

By following this guideline he had discovered that he was as much at peace when he took out the trash or washed the dishes or ironed his shirts as he was when he went out to dinner with friends or swam at the seashore.

29

"These are different experiences of peace," he said. "Yet each is complete and whole in itself and not pushing or rushing to become the other."

"Is it fair to be at peace so often, so much?" I asked.

Again, he laughed. "Absolutely," he said. "It's the fairest thing on earth. Granted, such a constant experience of peace is unusual, but it's perfectly lawful. In fact, my own experience has convinced me beyond doubt that enjoying peace is the first thing life calls us to do, the first gift life has to offer."

He said that shortly after his experience in the park the question of whether it was moral or right to be so devoted to peace had become a burning question for him. As the years went by he wondered whether it was appropriate to be enjoying such prolonged hours and days and weeks of quiet, uninterrupted peace while others were obviously experiencing similar weeks, months and even years of turmoil, of suffering, darkness and despair. The world news and his own clinical practice had presented him ample examples of such inner warfare and turmoil.

"First, it was quite easy to see that my own practice of peace was certainly neither the cause nor a contributing factor to the turmoil of others. It was also easy for me to see that whenever I *forgot* my peace, or neglected my discipline, and indulged in dark moods, fears, frustrations or self-pity, I did indeed cause more turmoil, unhappiness and suffering."

He said that he had entered clinical practice for the sole purpose of testing and sharing the practice of peace. Even after seven years of graduate work, and countless hours of clinical training, he knew that his own experience of peace was the basis of all that he had to offer. He could see that his own life had no passion, no color, no energy without a foundation in peace. He observed that when he neglected his discipline of peace, he was a drain on those around him.

"I decided that even if others thought it was unfair or crazy or politically incorrect for me to practice peace all the time, even still, the best thing I could do for them and for myself was to secretly remain true to my discipline. I had to be brave to do this, because I seemed to be doing it alone. And yet I saw that if I did not practice this discipline I would be adding to the world's unhappiness. I did not want to add any more unhappiness to the world. I wanted to make at least my little corner, my presence a bit brighter, easier, safer for those who came to it."

He said he was further convinced of the rightness of this strategy when he observed, with humility, that in a group setting if he himself remained attuned to the natural peace that such attunement was quietly infectious to almost every other member of the group. "My research has convinced me that peace is the native state of human beings," he said. "Peace is our natural state. So when I honor my own natural, native state, simply by remaining with it, then others likewise give themselves permission to do the same thing. No words need be exchanged about what we're doing."

Again, being in my materialist/existentialist graduate student frame of mind, I questioned him as to whether human beings truly were "natively, naturally at peace."

"I'm at peace with this view," he laughed. "If you are not at peace with these thoughts, you are not obliged to

31

think them. Enjoying your peace, being at peace with your thoughts, is the most important thing for you and for me, not whether you agree with the content of my thoughts."

"Is being at peace with our thoughts more important than the literal truth of the thoughts?" I asked.

"Truth is prior to thoughts," he said immediately. It was clear he had been thinking about this. "Peace will always lead you to the truth. The deepest truth. That has been my experience."

I was silent. His words had made me stop thinking for a moment, to look behind my thoughts.

"Truth, Love, Beauty, God, Principle, Spirit, Divinity, Existence — these are just words," he said. "What is the reality that these words point to?" At that moment he hit the arm of the chair he was sitting on several times. He continued, "The word 'chair' refers to this reality that is more than the word. So is there a *reality* behind these fancy words, or are they just made up words, pointing to nothing?"

"Sometimes, I think they're just made up," I confessed.

"Yes, of course, for some people who have not explored behind the words, they are," he agreed. "If not made up, then borrowed. They have no direct experience of the reality behind those words. For other people, they do not need the words, and certainly don't need to argue about the words, because their own direct experience of the reality behind the words, that the words are pointing to, is inarguable.

"So don't worry so much about the words," he said. "Put your awareness on your experience of peace, even if it's only a slight, tiny grain of peace, even if it's fleeting, put your attention there. That will be the leaven that raises the whole loaf. In my experience, the closer you are to your natural peace, the closer you are to your deepest truth. When you stray from your peace, you stray from truth."

That made sense to me. In that moment I saw that I didn't need to argue about truth, or God, or salvation because the reality behind those words — if there was a reality — would sooner or later reveal itself, or not. I saw how I might need to first experience peace before I could clearly see the wider reality around me. I told him I thought I understood, and asked him how I could quicken my practice.

Dr. Charlie said that the first step in training myself to constantly honor the presence of peace was to simply recognize the absolute *practicality* of being at peace in every relationship and in every circumstance. If I recognized how *practical* it was to have peace in my life, he said, then the importance of my practice of the simple methods we had discussed would become apparent. He said that as my recognition and understanding of the absolute practicality of living with peace was confirmed by the simple daily events in my life, then the energy of peace itself, which was larger than my own personal story, would begin to manifest, spontaneously moving me into the next steps for the maturation of my practice. He assured me that as I remained with the simple methods he shared with me then before long I would be able to access peace in almost everything I did, and I would do so spontaneously without effort or strain. (I have since discovered that he was right, of course. Otherwise I would not be sharing these notes!)

Dr. Charlie said that he was well aware of our fearful cultural superstition—stemming from our Puritan ancestors—that if we focus on enjoying our lives, being at peace with our lives, then at some future point we would have to "pay the piper" through some form of pain, depression or other misfortune, maybe even death itself. Our culture tells us, he observed, that if we are not to be punished later for all this peace and happiness in our lives then we should first work and sweat in order to deserve such a gift. We are told that as "fallen human beings" we are destined to long, hard, mostly un-peaceful and unhappy hours of work and sacrifice before we deserve to enjoy a little bit of natural peace.

"In our culture the experience of peace is assumed to be the end reward, not the daily means, of our personal activity," he said. "I no longer assume this. I don't believe it's true now and I don't believe it was ever true.

"Pain, misfortune, depression and death are already present around the world," he observed. "They clearly are not the result of too much peace in our lives. As I practice my discipline, and share it with others, I see pain, misfortune and depression falling away in their lives. In fact, I've seen how death itself no longer has a hold on us when we practice this discipline. Peace is the bridge between this world and the next. The bridge goes both ways."

I asked what he meant by that. He said that he had personally experienced how the presence of peace, which is at the root of consciousness, is what carries us from this world into the next. He said that not only does peace carry us into the next world, it is what is waiting for us there."

"You've been there?" I asked.

"Yes," he said, "Many times. Peace is our ticket into all the dimensions." He said that it is often the lack of peace on this side of the veil that moves people to drop their body and move on. "We want to be with our native state," he said. "We will do anything, including dropping the physical form, to be closer to it."

He said that contrary to cultural mis-belief, but nevertheless quite logically, practicing our peace always leads to more peace. He quoted scripture, "To them that have, it shall be added unto. To them that have not, it shall be taken away." When we practice enjoying peace in the moment, he said, practice being at peace with the thoughts we are thinking right now, we prepare the way for greater peace later in our lives. To ignore or deny our daily, momentary experience of peace—to indulge in thoughts right now that bring us turmoil and pain—simply prepares the way for more turmoil and pain. This simple wisdom suddenly made sense to me.

He said that when awkward or uncomfortable situations or relationships arose for him, as they naturally do for everyone, his method was to simply release, as best he could, the thoughts with which he was not at peace in relation to these situations or relationships and return to thoughts with which he was more at peace, thoughts either about the situation or about something completely different. He said that by doing so he inevitably found that peace itself gave him guidance and insight into the previously unpleasant circumstances, spontaneously propelling him to say and do the most appropriate thing.

He said that when he failed to be at peace with himself in such a circumstance or relationship, as everybody at some point does, his method was to consciously refrain from condemning himself for his failure to be at peace and instead, in that moment, simply again let peace invade his view—his thoughts—of himself, his history and his future. He said in this way he discovered it was never too late to be at peace with all the people and events in his life because peace itself has no time boundaries and can move forward and backward with equal ease. Hearing his words, I glimpsed how I, too, might change, enlighten my past, which until then, I had assumed was very tumultuous, very unhappy.

We were quiet for a while as I mulled over what he had been telling me. Then Dr. Charlie told me I was a very good listener, a very good student. "But we don't need to be so serious and heavy about this," he said.

He said he wanted to share with me some of the more playful ways of relating to peace that he had found to quicken his own practice. He said that he sometimes plays the inner game of separating himself from peace in order to talk to peace as he might talk to his own mother.

"I talk and she talks back," he said, grinning. "We have become very good friends. She is very tender, and funny and wise, and she supports and guides me as a very wise old mother might gently support and guide her grown son."

"That's kind of weird," I said, with a grin.

"Yes, isn't it!" he laughed. "Yet it is also easy and natural. Nothing is forbidden when you follow the promptings of peace!"

"Nothing?" I asked.

"Nothing," he said. "Because peace is always loving, never violent or cruel."

"Don't some people enjoy being cruel or violent?"

"My experience with people who are cruel and violent—and I have met many in my practice—is that such emotions and actions come about simply because they are *not* in touch with their peace, their joy. They want to feel alive, triumphant and free, and these aberrant behaviors are the only way they know to feel that way. They want to live an exciting life, focused in the moment. When they are taught an easier way, that lasts longer, feels better, their cruelty and violence always fall away. Always."

I had to take this on faith. It was something new. "Back to peace," I said. "What other games do you play?"

He looked at me curiously, as if questioning, and didn't respond for a moment. "Sometimes," he said at last, "I allow myself to be the mother—to be peace itself—an impersonal ocean of light and love. I let Dr. Charlie disappear. The only thing inside of me, or outside, beyond the far galaxies, is impersonal peace, love, joy. "

I stared at him, not knowing what to say.

He brought us back to earth.

"At other times I pretend to hold in the palm of my hand just one tiny grain of peace — the size of a mustard seed. With this little grain, I move mountains of doubt and distrust and suffering. I have discovered that there is no right or wrong way to play with peace," he said. "And I have also discovered that there is no difficulty that is outside of the powerful embrace of peace."

What he was saying was, again, stopping my mind. My thoughts were stalled. I could sense the beauty of his practice, and the truth of his words, and yet I had no intellectual response, no argument for or against. As I was simply enjoying his presence, I felt something profound shifting inside me.

"You, too, will discover your own ways to play with peace," he said. "And peace will find unique ways of playing with you! There is an old saying, *Take one step toward Allah, and Allah will take ten steps toward you.* When you consciously practice personal peace, impersonal peace will respond. It is the nature of peace to grow and manifest, be magnified, inside and out."

I believed him. I could see how it would happen. Over the years, I have found that his words came true. Still, at the time, I challenged him. I told him that I believed life had both light and dark, happiness and sorrow, times of peace and times of war and turmoil. I believed we had to take the good with the bad.

"My experience is that peace is that force which is present *before* either light or dark," he said. "Behind light and dark. Therefore, when we access it we spontaneously bring back a natural balance wherever we are. But I know what you're driving at, and I don't mean to argue. Let me give you a small example from my daily life."

He said he had been on his way to an important professional meeting at which he had been asked to be a consultant when his pickup truck broke down, wouldn't move, in the middle of a busy street. He had a sense of what the problem was — an electrical short from the distributor — and that it was not going to be easily fixed. He said that he found his thoughts about his meeting, the snarling traffic, the expense of repairs, the need to call a tow truck all backing up in his mind like a river suddenly blocked by a rockslide.

"I consciously let go of all these thoughts I was not at peace thinking," he said. "Even though they kept coming back around, again and again, like leaves caught in a whirlpool. The electrical system was shorted out and even my emergency flasher lights were not working. As I got out of my truck and waved the cars around, I consciously let go of thoughts that stressed me. I looked for just the simplest thing with which I might be at peace. As I waved people around my truck, I pretended they were my thoughts. Some were frustrated and angry at this brief inconvenience I had caused. Some were curious. Most were on their way to somewhere else and weren't engaged at all with this particular circumstance. This little game made me grin, and my grin seemed to help folks move easier around and through the small traffic jam I had caused. And then I caught a glimmer of beautiful soft yellow light coming in through the trees, bouncing off my truck. I knew the light started nine million miles away. Suddenly I was no longer upset with this circumscribed physical condition. I relaxed. Immediately after I relaxed, within moments, a man in the exact same model pickup stopped behind mine and asked if I needed help. He put his flashers on. Before he got back into his truck another car pulled into a driveway by the side of the road and four young Hispanic men got out and ran into the street to help me. With safety flashing lights going, we pushed my truck to the side of the road. I called a tow truck, which was fortunately not far away. Within a very short time he had arrived, and we were on our way to the garage. I was sitting up front with the driver, and noticed we just happened to pass the building where my meeting was being held. He stopped and let me out. I entered the meeting room, in somewhat of a flurry, at the exact moment perfect for saying and doing what needed to be said and done. In fact, my absence had allowed the meeting to take a direction it otherwise might not have taken.

"This is a very small example. But it works at all levels," he said. "The energy by which the universe runs is a peaceable energy. As we stay with our peace, reconnect with our peace, we stay in harmony with the flow of the universal energy. When we forget our peace, we quickly get tumbled about by the circumstances of our life."

He gave me another small example from his own daily life. He said that some years back he realized that he seldom enjoyed mowing his lawn. It was a chore that he had never seen as especially interesting, necessary or worthwhile. And it also seemed to bring back many unhappy and violent memories from his childhood. When he realized that this was an area where he was not at peace in his life he started by first *being at peace* with his dislike, being at peace with his resistance. He allowed himself to be at peace with the negative thoughts that had previously led to irritation and frustration with the lawnmower and the chore itself. "I imagined blowing up the lawnmower," he said. "I could be at peace with that thought. Then I imagined blowing up the lawn itself. I imagined blowing up the whole block. And then I imagined having a tiny patch of lawn six inches wide and six feet long that I could mow in less than two minutes." He said he indulged in these fantasies as he was mowing his lawn. His peace training included giving himself permission to be at peace with himself just as he was, with all the faults and weaknesses he had accumulated, which in that instance included his dislike for mowing the lawn. So he chose to be at peace with his dislike.

While engaging the chore itself, he continued with his method of selecting only thoughts with which he was at peace, and letting go of thoughts with which he was not at peace. "Sometimes I was at peace not mowing the lawn for three or four weeks," he said. He said that by giving authority to his peace rather than to his obligation to mow the lawn, there were many, many times when his lawn became shaggy and ill kept. But as

41

he continued with his discipline he discovered an unexpected softening and then a complete dissolution of his inner resistance. And a falling away of the unpleasant memories from childhood.

"Lawn mowing is now a very peaceable chore for me," he said. "I am as much at peace mowing the lawn as I am sitting by a mountain lake or attending a conference in Hawaii. My peace does not depend on what I am doing or not doing."

"Why didn't you just hire someone to mow the lawn?" I asked.

"I did that, too," he said. "And now that I am at peace when mowing the lawn, I will probably hire someone again. But at the time I found myself troubled by my thoughts about these young men, and sometimes women, working a chore that I myself would not do, or did not enjoy to do. We are, after all, brothers and sisters. When I asked them about their jobs, most of them confessed that they enjoyed the money but did not especially enjoy the work itself. So even though the lawn was getting mowed, the work itself was not getting done. You know what I mean?"

I understood, yes.

"I give this example of mowing the lawn to make it simple," he said. "But I have successfully worked the same process with clients who were dealing with the most difficult of life issues, from incest and murder to terminal disease and bankruptcy. In every case, the work is the same. And it's always an inner work."

Still, I understood.

For some reason, I then asked him if he prayed, or meditated. "Yes, sure" he said, "quite regularly. But I admit that I no longer can tell much difference between the state of mind that I experience during prayer and mediation and the state of mind that I experience throughout the day."

"What state is that?" I asked.

"Peace and joy, of course!" he laughed. He said he spent time almost every morning in prayer and meditation, and occasionally in the evenings. During these periods he simply directed his attention to peaceable thoughts of God, or Love, Joy, and found himself "at home" without motivation to go anywhere else. "But I do pretty much the same thing during all of my day life," he laughed. "I guess it's because I've learned how enjoyable it is to think thoughts with which I am at peace rather than thoughts with which I'm not at peace. Peace, or joy, is always available. You can tell when you're accessing it, because you're grinning."

I laughed. "So you grin while you're praying, or meditating?" I asked.

"Sure!" he said. "That's the only way I know I'm connected and that it's working."

"That's the kind of mediation or prayer I'd like to do," I said.

He smiled, and simply nodded his head. "That's the kind I teach," he said, softly.

We sat in silence for a moment. As an agnostic existentialist, I felt a bit awkward dealing with prayer and meditation, so I changed the subject and asked him how he related his personal practice to his professional responsibilities. He said there was no difference. He had discovered that sharing the simple methods he himself used for accessing peace dissolved all need for employing other therapeutic remedies. He said he did occasionally use more complex approaches when he wanted to encourage more fun and light-heartedness with particular clients, though for his seriously disturbed, injured or dangerous clients he always remained completely dedicated to teaching them to directly access peace itself, which he knew to be the most basic and efficient curative, balancing agent.

"I feel I owe it to my clients to offer them the most direct access to their own peace of mind," he said. "This is what they come to me for. They want to experience more peace in their lives, more joy. I show them in the first session how to do that.

"I don't' want to sound like I am a saint, or that I have all the answers," he said. "In both my personal and professional life I am continually being tempted away from peace. And I do not always resist the temptation!" He laughed, and I laughed with him,

He said that the intensity of his awareness of peace naturally varied from moment to moment, even though he knew that the peace itself was absolute, unvarying. He said that he did not let the rising and falling of his awareness of peace be a cause for doubt or self-deprecation. He said that over the years his awareness of the presence of peace had steadily increased, and that now in his mature years the waxing and waning was in fact much more subtle than it had been previously.

"I take comfort in knowing that peace itself—that which I am accessing—is an absolute presence," he repeated. "Peace itself never dims or brightens. It's only my own awareness of it coming and going that makes it seem as though it does."

I asked him what he did when he caught himself not paying much attention to the background peace.

"I laugh," he said. "I grin. "

"On purpose?" I asked.

"Sometimes on purpose, but mostly spontaneously, when I see the suffering I am causing myself in that moment. I have learned to be at peace with my own foibles, my human proclivity and fascination with suffering and unhappiness, in all its forms."

"So you just laugh at it?"

"I laugh at myself. I take myself lightly. And then, when I see what I've been doing, I stop doing it. I consciously move my attention away from the thoughts that are causing the turmoil to thoughts with which I am more at peace. Or I simply choose to be at peace with the thoughts that a moment before were causing me trouble. It's my basic, constant practice. It's so simple, and yet it does require practice. It is simple, but not easy, especially at the beginning, since we have been trained in the other direction."

He said he was now seldom tempted to believe that his experiences of trouble or frustration or disappointment arise from some outside force, or circumstance or relationship. Rather, he knows that such a dimming of happiness is inevitably because of some *story* he is inwardly creating, rehearsing, and enlarging upon in regards to this exterior force, circumstance or relationship. His solution now is always to change the inner story, or to change his approach to the inner story so that he might more easily be at peace with it. He said that he was now consistently focused on the support of peace in his own thought rather than in trying to change or develop or unlock some outer circumstance. By focusing solely on peace in his own thought, he said, he found that the outer circumstances began to change on their own, would develop, unlock.

"Sometimes we are forced to think thoughts that are not peaceable," I argued. "What about all the wars and poverty and suffering going on? Either on a large scale or in our own personal lives. Are you saying we just ignore them?"

He paused for a long moment. "No. 'Course not," he said softly. "Like everyone else, in both my personal life and professional life, I can not help but be deeply aware of the suffering and pain and unhappiness that seem so rampant here among humans. So obviously our work here on earth is to help dissolve this wide unhappiness, for ourselves and others, as quickly and permanently as we can. Where to begin?"

"It's a big problem," I said.

"We begin with what we are thinking," he said. "We begin with the poverty, the wars, the suffering in our own thought stream. My experience after many, many years with this discipline is that we are *never* obliged to think in ways that add to the wars, the turmoil, to the suffering. We are often tempted, yes. But never obliged."

"Hmmm...." I said.

"How do we guide ourselves, and the world, out of war and poverty and suffering?" he asked.

"Good question," I said.

"It is a good question," he agreed. "I am proposing an experiment that we follow peace itself—through following thoughts with which we are peace—see where they lead. When we experiment in this way, when we follow peace itself, even just a little by managing our thoughts, soon we will learn to trust the process completely, because those thoughts with which we are at peace can be trusted, and always lead us to do the right thing at the right time."

It seemed a stretch. Maybe good in theory, but such a steady peace in our lives seemed unreasonable, ungrounded.

"The thoughts with which you are not at peace," he said. "Will these make better guides?"

"Probably not," I agreed.

"I have learned that every thought that troubles me is an unnecessary and inefficient thought," he said. "I have learned that thoughts that trouble me do not serve my body, or my family, or my clients or society. Troubling thoughts arise, of course, but we don't need to give them any energy, any allegiance. They are like weeds, simply not useful."

I was having a hard time believing what I was hearing. It was almost inconceivable that Dr. Charlie could be so dedicated, so disciplined and so brave in this practice of peace. And so precise, that he could filter out troubling thoughts.

It seemed as if he could tell the tenor of what I was thinking. He told me then that in the early years of his practice he often found himself, like everybody else, chewing and rehearsing thoughts and stories that were troubling, with which he was not at peace. He said his practice was to consciously reject these thoughts and stories only to discover that he was quite quickly chewing on them, rehearsing them again. Nevertheless, he continued in his practice day after day and soon noticed that his capacity for peace was expanding. His struggle to dismiss or re-contextualize troubling thoughts began to diminish. After a while, it was not such a struggle.

"At some point," he said, "I realized the struggle had gone. I was consistently grounded in peace. Peace had become my ordinary, moment by moment experience."

"How long did that take?" I asked.

"One second!" he laughed. "That's how long it takes to return to peace. One second at a time, over many years! And then you no longer need a second. You're already there."

He said that contrary to popular therapeutic theory and practice, he no longer believed it necessary or useful for his clients to dredge up old sorrows or traumas or unhappy memories in order to heal them or release them. He said that he now always encouraged his clients to go directly to peace itself, using the methods we had discussed.

"As Gandhi said, 'the means and the ends are the same,'" Dr. Charlie said. "So if the end, the goal of a therapeutic relationship is the client's increased enjoyment of life, and the acquisition of tools and skills to maintain that joy regardless of the circumstances, then why not get down to business from the start?"

Now it was my turn to laugh. I did, and quickly agreed.

He said that he had discovered that within the presence of peace was an intelligence, and power, and a "living energy" beyond that which we as individuals can consciously generate. When we hold to the peace residing in consciousness we are therefore holding this wider intelligence, this wider power, this presence that is more than ourselves.

"In fact, to be linguistically precise," he said, "We don't hold peace in consciousness. It is peace that is holding us, holding our consciousness, our awareness. These are the arms we are nestled in, though like infants, we seldom realize our wondrous position."

He said that he had discovered that as we follow our individual awareness of peace, as we take up the discipline of peace, however clumsily or fitfully we might at first do it, that by such practice we are thereby moved into the larger arena where our daily lives take on more service to others. He said that by practicing this individual discipline we are more precisely aligned with the larger forces of the universe, and thus we spontaneously serve, support and exhibit the universal, transcendental artistry already here unfolding.

"Wow," I said. "The universal, transcendental artistry."

He laughed. "These words just come out of me. It's what I observe."

"That's nice work, if you can get it," I said.

"We don't need to concern ourselves about the universal, transcendental artistry at work," he said. "It's much simpler than that. We just concern ourselves with what we are thinking, as we take out the trash, whether we are peace or not."

Our session was coming to a close. He reiterated that the path to peace always begins with peace itself — the means and the ends are the same. We are at peace when we entertain thoughts and stories with which we are peace. We are not at peace when we entertain and give energy to troubling thoughts.

He said that for many people the thoughts and stories of Jesus or Buddha or Allah or Krishna or some other life teacher or teaching were the doorways by which they discovered the peace in their consciousness, and that these entrances were perfectly appropriate, useful and wise. In his professional practice he had observed that those who had vigorously sought peace through outer physical stimulations or emotional relationships or social acceptances and advancements were often those most relieved and enchanted by this path to peace through simple inner cognitive adjustments.

On the other hand, he had observed that those who had been hesitant about accepting peace or comfort or joy from without — generally because of their cultural or religious training — had often trained themselves to be likewise hesitant about accepting the same from within. In either case, however, the practice of the presence of peace was sufficient to eventually bring about balance and enlightenment, e.g., an increasingly peaceable and happy life.

He assured me that my pleasure in the world around me would intensify, and that my awareness of the inner peace would grow ever deeper as I continued with the practice of consciously entertaining only those thoughts with which I was at peace—consciously changing, or releasing those thoughts that troubled me. "But I don't want you to take my word for it," he said. "Just become curious as to whether or not what I say might work for you. Take up the experiment with your own thoughts. Begin with the thoughts you are thinking right now."

He said that as I intensified my practice I would soon discover that my awareness of peace was less and less dependent on outer relationships, possessions or events. He said that since my peace did not depend on these outer things I would discover that I was increasingly feeling less and less threatened, and that my fears would fall away, my worries dissolve. In such a peaceable frame of mind, he said, my service to others naturally, spontaneously improved.

"This all sounds pretty good," I had to admit.

He laughed. "It is! The best part, however, is that you yourself don't have to do hardly anything. It's peace itself that is working in you. You simply let peace do what it wants to do."

"There's still a part of me that sees this practice as just a great excuse for doing anything I want, like drugs, sex and rock and roll," I said. "It seems it could easily lead to more selfishness and self-indulgence."

He was again quiet for a moment. I thought maybe I had offended him, or he was disappointed that I had not caught the essence of his message. When he broke his silence, he surprised me.

"There's nothing wrong with drugs, sex or rock and roll," he said. "Nothing is forbidden, personally or communally. When we use peace as our guide, we are no longer confined by cultural or tribal customs or taboos."

"Wow." I said again.

He giggled and assured me that I was free to sleep in the sun or play in the woods or watch movies in my room for days on end, if this is what peace led me to do.

"That's great to know," I said. "I hope my professors agree."

"Whether they agree or not," he said, "You're still free!"

I realized that was true.

"Don't worry," he said. "My experience is that when we actually practice peace we spontaneously do what's best for us to do. Without even trying we fulfill our responsibilities, and follow the most valuable social norms and expectations, while ignoring the silly or superstitious expectations. Following peace often leads us to spontaneously set even higher social standards. My experience is that as we practice the presence of peace, we find ourselves being *more* productive, *more* prosperous, *more* ethical and upright than when we don't."

Again, what he was saying made sense.

He reminded me that many people are already secretly or openly involved in self-pleasuring and selfish struggling. They aren't following some disciplined "peace training" for such activities. In fact, relying on such pursuits they find that their peace is always very fleeting. And their frustrations often lead to violence and un-love. He said that as we practice accessing the peace that resides within us, we are completely free to move about in the world, to explore, to experience and taste the world as it unfolds. But we are not dependent on such explorations for what is most important to us, and what is already close at hand – our innate ability to live in peace.

"Ahh, so this is how we can be in the world, but not of it," I said.

"Yes, through our practice of peace, we fulfill the scriptures," he laughed.

He said that my practice of magnifying the presence of peace would attract power for me to do well in this world, including doing well with my professors, and to do good for others and myself. He said that it was the lack of true peace in people's lives that led to selfish debauchery, dishonesty and decay.

"A soul hungers and thirsts for that which is most true," he said. "In religious terms, I have discovered that peace is the sign of the Christ. It is the Staff of Life, the Brahman, the Tao, the Buddha Mind. On this you can lean all your days!"

I grinned. With these last words, I was completely full, to overflowing. I couldn't fit any more in. He knew it. I knew it. Our lengthy, life-changing (for me) second session had come to an end. We stood. Shook hands. I thanked him deeply. In the decades since he first spoke these words to me I have discovered the truth behind his words has appeared in my life again and again. For this, I am deeply grateful.

Third Conversation:
Peace is the Whole Enchilada

I had been very moved by our second conversation, and in the weeks that followed found myself spontaneously engaged in the discipline—entertaining thoughts with which I was at peace, dropping or re-contextualizing the thoughts that troubled me. I had caught a glimpse of the how practical it is, for myself and those around me, when I practice living peaceably. A new light was dawning in my life.

In our third conversation, which took place several weeks later, I shared with Dr. Charlie my new appreciation for the importance of peace in our lives. It was certainly not something I had learned in graduate school. He laughed, and agreed, and told me again that the focus of his own life—other than the practice itself—was an intellectual and philosophical conviction of the practicality of peace in both his secular and spiritual pursuits. It was a conviction that was continuously being confirmed in all his life experiences.

55

On the secular side, he said that as a psychotherapist he knew that those who came to him did so with the simple hope that he could help them experience more peace, more happiness, more fulfilling relationships, more relaxed social movement, greater prosperity and less inner turmoil. He said he always pointed his clients to their inner reservoir of peace, and showed them again and again how to access this reservoir. Doing so, he said, had time and again fulfilled his clients' expectations in coming to him.

"It is peace itself that is doing the work," he laughed. "Yet I'm the one who gets paid!"

I assured him it was worth his fee to find the key that unlocks this inner reservoir. I told him I was still not sure about the spiritual terminology or dimensions that he mentioned.

"It's quite simple," he said. "My understanding is that the word 'Peace' and the word 'Christ' are two words pointing to the same Presence."

"Ahh," I said.

"Also 'Peace' and 'Allah' are two words pointing to the same Supreme Being. 'Peace' and *atman* are two words for the same reality. Peace and the Tao. The Creator is a Peaceable Presence. Peace is the door to Spirit."

"In other words, peace can be another word for the whole enchilada," I said.

"Yes, exactly," he laughed. "The whole enchilada. You can call it *enchilada* if that suits you best. You don't need the other words if they don't suit your own tradition. In my own case, when I realized that the presence of peace and the spiritual reality are one in the same, like water and wet, I found it easier, intellectually, philosophically, to stay with this practice of remaining with peace. Knowing that practicing peace was okay with the God of Abraham, Moses and Jesus, I finally had permission to stay with peace, practice peace, through all of my days and nights, waking, dreaming or sleeping."

He reminded me again that direct access to peace was through either a.) Dropping those thoughts and stories we don't enjoy or are troublesome and finding or creating ones with which we are more at peace; or b.) Deciding to be at peace with the thoughts and stories that a moment before were troubling us.

"It's simple," he said, "Kids do this all the time. But for us adults, trained to think about what we don't enjoy, to think about what troubles us, the peace practice is simple but not easy, at least in the beginning."

He also said that when he found that he was again thinking thoughts that troubled him he made a point of not condemning or berating or belittling himself for not staying with his peace. Rather, he simply determined to be at peace with the fact that he had forgotten, at peace with the fact that he had momentarily strayed from his practice.

"We humans are crazy when we do this," he said, "forget to do what is the most necessary and practical thing we can do in any circumstance or relationship. To beat ourselves up for forgetting our peace just prolongs the craziness!" He had discovered that to be at peace with having forgotten was the most direct route back to peace.

I told him that as I practiced accessing the presence of peace, in the manner he was suggesting, that I sometimes felt as though I was moving alone against the tide, moving contrary to all my learning, and to all my culture, fighting the whole system.

"Yes, often you are!" he agreed. "We are not trained to access peace. We are trained, mostly by example, to complain and worry."

He said that the courage to abandon our complaints and to abandon the slights against us, and to abandon our feelings of being insulted and offended — such courage to abandon turmoil and unhappiness is within us naturally, given by God, although such courage is often sleeping, or dormant. He assured me that as I exercised my courage, stayed with my practice, that the world would open up wider and brighter, and that the whole human culture and all its institutions would eventually bend to support and serve my further practice.

"But don't wait for the culture, or the systems to bend to your practice, "he said. "You have already experienced that the presence of peace is its own reward. Your experience of peace is always confirmed by an *immediate* sense of release and ease. You don't need to wait for weeks or months or years for the rewards of this practice. The rewards are always immediately experienced. And they are cumulative."

He said that the intensity of my experience of peace will be sometimes greater and sometimes lesser as I practice letting go of the various turmoils and long standing complaints in my day life. Still, he assured me that my overall awareness of peace would continue to increase as I employed these methods, regardless of where I started.

He said that by accessing the presence of peace I would always be led to perform the most appropriate actions, at just the right time. He said that his experience of this principle, or law, was so consistent that in all the large and small matters of both his personal and professional life he trusted that peace would, as the scriptures say, "Go before him to make the crooked places straight." And it always did.

He said that by staying with peace, by thinking and saying and doing what he was most at peace thinking, saying and doing, he was always supplied with the right words, the right gestures, the right friends and helpmates to make daily living smooth, bright and beautiful. He said that he knows that such daily grace is not an accident or result of mere good fortune but rather the absolute power of peace itself.

He said that in his own life he has found the presence of peace so consistently available that whenever he finds himself temporarily or momentarily lost in the drabness or neutrality or the listlessness of daily events, he now habitually returns his attention to thoughts with which he is secretly at peace — be they positive, negative, scatological or other-worldly — and thereby discovers the return of his natural buoyancy. He said that he was now so consistently delighted with his daily tasks and daily relationships and professional duties that he had to consciously remind himself to move out of one and into the next because he was so often aware that each moment presented itself as complete and perfect and in no need of either addition or subtraction.

"I have been shown, and have demonstrated, that peace is my own natural state," he said. "And I am convinced that peace is likewise the natural state of every other human being."

Such an understanding allows him to be as peaceable and at ease in fulfilling his daily routines and obligations as when he is engaged in forms of recreation or social entertainment or when he was engaged in personal prayers and meditation. "They are different expressions, different qualities of peace in different circumstances," he said. "Yet the root is the same. Connected with the root, I am equally at peace in all of these moments."

He said that he had experienced peace in so many different modes, with so many different people under so many different circumstances, and while in so many different states of bodily comfort or discomfort, that he was quite sure that peace would accompany him — or that he would accompany it — for the rest of his physical life and that he would continue with it even when his physical body no longer contained him. Indeed, he said, his physical body even now no longer contained him, and he was aware from personal experience that peace remains accessible to all of us no matter what domain, subtle or gross, we might journey through.

He said that he had come to see that presence of peace is the presence of the universe itself; the presence of both heaven and earth, and all the subtle and gross levels of consciousness. Therefore, he was now convinced that this presence was his most suitable focus of study and the most consistent and worthy companion. He said that this understanding had proven itself accurate again and again in every conceivable form.

"What about all the pain and suffering in the world," I asked. "How can we be naturally at peace when there seems to be so much proof of warfare, suffering and death?"

He said that he was of course very aware of what the world considered to be pain, suffering, hardship and sorrow. Still, his own experience confirmed the power of peace — the power of God — to dissipate all such appearances, all such conditions, and the testimony of scripture in all cultures upheld his intuition, as did the lives of those who devoted themselves to the transcendental calm which accompanied his daily discipline. "How do we relieve the suffering in the world except by practicing non-suffering?" he asked.

"Non-suffering?"

"Joy, love, peace, when practiced as a discipline, rather than a hoped-for result, is the practice of non-suffering," he said. "Such a discipline heals both the small and large sufferings of the world. It shows such suffering is less real than the reality of God, of peace."

He said that this conviction, based on long personal experience, on occasion met with such disbelief that others would want to argue against or deny such peaceful possibilities. Most often, in such encounters, he felt neither need nor inclination to debate the matter, and instead simply remained at peace with the others' protestations, much as a mother remains at peace with the momentary protestations of her suckling babe while she moves him from one breast to the other. He said he was no longer willing to go away from the presence of peace even long enough to debate the efficacy of peace or prove its efficiency. He said that because of his practice he was already immersed in the wholeness of peace, and thus felt no urge to try to gain more peace through winning arguments or making converts or impressing others with his state. He said he felt he was experiencing the Presence of God when he experienced the presence of peace and therefore he experienced heaven on earth as a daily reality. He said that even if the word peace and the word God were not two words for the same Presence, even still, he was convinced that God would use the presence of peace to reveal to His (Her) children His (Her) will for them. Dr. Charlie said he was not interested in or devoted to any God who would deny peace or demand use of some other means for communication. He said the God he had come to know was Absolute Love, Absolute Joy, Absolute Peace, and that this was sufficient divinity for him.

Dr. Charlie again reiterated that his simple methods for accessing peace—choosing only the inner "stories," or thoughts with which he was at peace, and immediately dropping the stories, or thoughts that troubled him, or just changing his mood toward them—such simple methods were immediately verifiable by an immediate increase in an awareness of peace. Although one's skill in accessing and maintaining this awareness of peace improved and deepened with practice, the methods did not require long practice to begin offering fruits.

"Any person may begin feeling more peace immediately simply by choosing thoughts which are more peaceable, or by choosing to not fight the thoughts to which culture or habit would deny such peace."

"What if we can't find any peaceful thoughts to enjoy?" I asked.

"First, as you observe your own thoughts, you will discover that thoughts themselves are neither peaceful nor un-peaceful," he said. "It's a subtle point, but very powerful. Thoughts are just thoughts. You are either at peace with the thought or you're not. The thoughts you choose to be at peace with or spontaneously enjoy, I may not enjoy, may not be at peace with. And the thoughts I'm at peace with, you may find troublesome."

I remembered that he had mentioned this before. "Okay, yes. So what if I can't find any thoughts I'm at peace with?"

"Just start with the thoughts you are thinking," he said. "Tweak them, play with them so that you are less troubled by them than you were a moment before. Then you are on the right path."

He said that such a peace-based discipline with one's thoughts did not, contrary to popular myth, lead an individual away from reality, but rather led one deeper into reality. He said that such simple methods were in fact the essence of the teachings of Jesus, Buddha, the Prophet and all the saints and sages who taught the path of love and compassion.

"The Great Tradition of spiritual awakening, in whatever form it takes around the world and through the ages, is in fact founded on and activated by love, which I understand is the presence of peace," he said. "Without love, without peace there is no spiritual awakening, regardless of any other exercises, disciplines, or knowledge engaged." He said that the barbarities and intolerances and enslavements that have been perpetrated under the name of religion have resulted from a mistaken separation, or demotion of love, or peace—from the spiritual framework. He said that as one practiced returning to the presence of peace in one's personal life, even without knowing the scriptural underpinnings of such a practice, that all traditions are nevertheless fulfilled in that one.

"Peace itself is a simple and natural presence," he said. "We do not need long treatises and intricate training to access this presence. We do, however, need to be brave and we need to be consistent in our devotion to it if we are to unlock all its potentials in our individual lives."

His words were again setting my mind at ease. I didn't need to go anywhere, be anywhere else than right where I was. Dr. Charlie's presence made it easy to see the truth of what he was teaching.

He said that as I trusted the presence of peace to guide my thoughts in the smaller details of my life, my experience with it would gently lead me into greater and greater reliance on it for my life's larger decisions and directions and involvements. He said that I would soon come to trust the power and wisdom of peace.

I said that I was learning to trust it already, and that his influence had been of great help to me. He said that our journey to peace is normally quickened when we are in community with others who are likewise practicing peace, although nothing stands in the way of gaining all fruits though the solitary engagements of these practices. He said, however, that one's individual practice of peace inevitably leads to the uplifting of all mankind, and therefore it is truly impossible to practice alone.

As our session came to a close, he reaffirmed that my first weeks and months practicing the discipline of peace would inevitably lead me into deeper and deeper experiences and expressions of peace. I would soon discover that peace was present and available when I was alone or in community, whether I was experiencing wealth or scarcity. I would find it in my vocation and in my avocations.

"If you look for the presence of peace in all of your circumstances and relationships," he said, as we got up to go, "all of your circumstances and relationships will be enlightened affairs."

"I like that," I said.

"Yes, me too," he agreed.

Simply being in his presence, hearing his words, experiencing their immediacy, I had no choice but to believe him completely. I could feel the truth of what he was saying deep in my psyche.

Fourth Conversation:
Even the Galaxies Bow Down to Peace

In our fourth session together Dr. Charlie once again talked openly and cheerfully with me about both his private and professional practices and his methods for accessing peace. It felt as though anything I wanted to ask him, about any area of his life, he was always willing and tickled to share with me. It seemed he lived his life without secrets. (He was equally free, open and spontaneously transparent throughout all the years of our friendship.)

"It's basically a matter of having the courage and willingness to simply release any thoughts we are troubled by and to stop telling all those inner stories which we do not enjoy hearing," he said. "We can abandon such thoughts, such stories, even without bringing them to some kind of resolution. The practice is to *immediately* think thoughts with which we are more at peace, and to tell ourselves only those stories which we are happy to hear, happy to tell. This is a moment by moment, hour by hour engagement with peace. This is a brave and enlightened way of living, and not, as culturally taught, a false or illusory view of existence."

Dr. Charlie once again assured me that peace is in fact my true nature, my native energy, and that although I might sometimes ignore this peace, or forget it or cover it up, it nevertheless remained with me as my basic energy. "This is why you can always immediately access the presence of peace no matter how long you may have been away from it."

He said that the presence of peace would always be the most reliable beacon for navigating the paths of my life. He said that when I was unsure about which direction to go or which actions to perform or not perform, I should listen for my sense of peace and it would consistently provide me with the most appropriate, most wise, fruitful and harmonious steps to take.

"Won't this just lead to laziness or further self-indulgence?" I asked. "I might be at peace just watching tv and drinking beer all day."

He laughed and nodded his head. "This is always the fear. That is why you must be courageous in testing it out. My experience is that when you follow the nudging of peace, it leads to just the right amount of self-indulgence, at just the right time. We are not forbidden to indulge ourselves in life's wondrous pleasures."

He said that as I turned again and again to the thoughts which I enjoyed thinking, and consistently dropped thoughts that troubled me, that this practice would lead me to a point where all of my actions were performed spontaneously for the simple joy of performance rather than because of some hoped for reward or pleasure. In this way, I would be moving efficiently in the world but not be ensnared seeking its false rewards or pleasures. I would be rewarded, he said, but with the *true* "gift" of being able to experience increasing pleasure from my work, and from my daily chores, my friends and family. From this gift, he assured me, all other gifts would emerge.

He said that by my constant releasing of thoughts that troubled me, abandoning my unhappy stories, I would be simultaneously acknowledging and honoring my innate spirit—my native peace—and thus I would be performing the fundamental discipline which is the basis for all human progress. By recognizing and practicing the presence of peace, he said, we accept our spirituality, our innate transcendental identity.

He said I did not need to feel discouraged when I forgot to practice. He said that the most appropriate response when I had forgotten about the presence of peace, or when my circumstances or relationships seemed to temporarily overwhelm or diminish my ability to access the presence, the most appropriate response was to simply move on, abandoning, as well as I could, the thoughts or stories which would darken my inner atmosphere. Instead, I was to simply take up whatever thoughts or stories would lighten, to even a small degree, this same inner territory. He reminded me then of the scriptural story of the mountains being removed by one who has the faith as small as a mustard seed. Such is the power of a single grain of peace—removing mountains of sorrow.

"Peace is the presence of Christ," he said. "Peace is Emmanuel, the *satori*, the *atman*, the divine spark which God has placed within every human. Even the galaxies must bow down to it." He said that the experience of peace is available to every human in every circumstance, in every relationship, in every economic and social condition which may arise or in which we might find ourselves. He said that he had proved this—witnessed this—over and over in his own life, and he had likewise witnessed it in every client and friend who had employed the same methods.

Like everybody, he said, in the beginning of his training he would occasionally allow his thoughts to drift into patterns which were troubling or upsetting. He confessed, however, that he had now grown so accustomed to living with peace that when it was not present he was very quick and very adept at recognizing such a turbulent state and spontaneously re-engaging his simple methods, and practices, which unfailingly returned him to the awareness of peace, his ordinary happy state.

He assured me that he did not consider himself to be constitutionally different from anyone else. He said that peace is always available to everyone, and easily accessible, especially after we have attained the intellectual and emotional understanding that honoring the presence of peace truly is the most practical thing we can do for ourselves and all those around us.

"The presence of peace does not depend on what you are doing, or who you are doing it with, or on what you own or where you live, but rather simply on your own inner thoughts about these outer conditions. As you choose those thoughts about these matters which you enjoy, with which you are peace, and drop the thoughts which trouble you or you don't enjoy, you will inevitably discover that there is no necessity to change *anything* whatsoever outside yourself in order to experience more peace. However, once you begin operating in this fashion you will discover that outer things in your life *do* change in consistently happy ways."

I asked him why it happened that way. He said that his own philosophical understanding was that by attending to peace we are attending to the universal energy that upholds the universe itself. The Peace Presence is the centering and empowering force of life. When we magnify our awareness of peace, life unfolds within and around us in much greater harmony.

He said that he used his own sudden experience of the presence of peace—which often was expressed in a spontaneous grin—as a sign that that his prayers had "hit home." He said he used the same spontaneous sign to indicate the wholeness and appropriateness of his actions. In his own life he had come to a point where he knew that the absence of this accompanying sign— the absence of a spontaneous grin, a happy release of tension—that neither his prayers nor his actions were yet complete. He said that it had become a simple matter for him to rest in peace, both in times of activity and inactivity, in exhilaration and in repose, with others or alone. He confirmed that his own awareness of peace was constant, though variably expressed and experienced. He said he had learned to enjoy the presence of peace when it was quiet, calm and un-extraordinary, as well as when it was boisterous, rushing and wild.

He said that contrary to many of our cultural traditions and religious teachings, we could in fact wholly trust our own awareness of peace to lead us into greater and greater awareness, into deeper and wider peaceable-ness. He suggested that, contrary to first appearances, it is in fact a *lack* of this trust in our own experience of peace, a lack of daily familiarity with this native state that leads to indulgent excesses and imbalances in life. Excessive drinking, sexual promiscuity and indulgences of every kind arise from a *narrowed* sense of peace—a limited ability to access peace. He said that as we recognize and return authority to our inner awareness of the presence of peace, the authority of outer addictions diminishes.

He urged me to engage the peace practice while performing each of the daily obligations and responsibilities which both my school life and home life required of me. In fact, he said, my challenge was specifically to transform all of what I now consider to be *burdens*—or chores—into peaceable pleasures. "Your daily round of feeding your pets and washing your clothes and cleaning the kitchen, paying bills, answering letters, weeding the garden, filing papers, preparing reports—all these are opportunities to practice accessing peace."

He said he recognized that I might not feel, at least in the beginning, that I was wholly succeeding in accessing the deepest peace as I went about my daily responsibilities. Nevertheless, he said, with practice and perseverance in the simple methods he had suggested, he was confident I would develop greater and greater skill in performing all of my duties with lightness and ease. "At some point you will recognize that peace is the most natural of companions, and your consistent helpmate." He said that by constantly returning to peace—through thinking thoughts and stories with which I was at peace and dropping or changing those which were troubling—I would inevitably be led to the experience of peace in all of my outer daily affairs. At this point, he said, my life would be radiating the peace and prosperity which spontaneously uplifts the entire world.

He suggested that with the peace practice, all the other virtues and strengths commonly associated with an upright life are automatically, effortlessly exhibited. With peace comes patience, confidence, truthfulness, tolerance, generosity, sincerity, sensibility and relational responses which are quick and appropriate. With the practice of peace we are aligned inwardly and outwardly with the rhythms and patterns of the universe. Such a practice leads us to recognize and experience our unity with life itself. "When we rest in peace," he said, "we express the universal completeness. We are individual expressions, manifestations of the infinitely loving, artistic beauty behind all of life."

"Well put," I said, and laughed. It was so simple. I could easily see, understand what he was saying, and it made so much sense.

He said that one who knows the presence of peace knows no social barriers. One who knows the presence of peace begins to transcend all human limitations and dissolve all hindrances. He said that by engaging the peace practice we naturally express Divine Love, and offer human hope and practical understanding to all who come into our sphere. He said that from the presence of peace all other transcendent qualities are derived.

I believed him and knew that he was pointing to something very true, but still I played the devil's advocate. I asked about the influence of greed and fear and pride and selfish ambition, which seemed rampant in our world. What about the wars and famine and natural catastrophes?

Dr. Charlie said that while locked into the time and space continuum of our earthly point of view we might assume peace and war, joy and sorrow, to be equal cohabitants, but that as we practice peace we discover the one to be wholly true and the other completely false. He said practicing peace leads inevitably to the transcending of our limited, cultural point of view, and to seeing in its stead the presence of heaven and its eternal formations, "regardless of what the physical senses might report."

For example, he said that as I began practicing peace, I would view my personal history with a different awareness, and thus my personal history would be transformed. He said that I would discover that I am now — and always have been and always will be — irrevocably encoded by and with life's beautiful undying essence.

"Seems hard to believe," I said.

"Keep practicing," he encouraged. "You'll see your awareness of peace expanding. As you see it unfolding in your own life, you'll find it easy to believe."

He said that I would see that an awareness of undying peace is in fact both my birthright and my destiny. He assured me that I was designed to live gracefully, effortlessly, in health and harmony, with ever-increasing wisdom and insight, good humor and peaceable-ness. He said that peace presence is the essence of the power behind all natural evolution, and thus by practicing peace we are granted spontaneous mastery over all the creation.

He said that my understanding would mature to a point where I would come to accept my happy, peaceable fortunes not as aberrant, undeserved occurrences, but rather as pre-ordained blessings lawfully accompanying unstoppable spiritual unfolding. He said that my own awareness of peace was an awareness of the peace in everybody and that "what blesses one blesses all." He advised me that my own spiritual unfolding was the unfolding of all the human races. Dr. Charlie said I could accept and expect that increasing daily happiness and unexpected opportunities for wider service to others would be the natural result of my practice. He said none of this required any effort because my work was simply to bear testimony to the already present peaceable

74

condition that is itself supporting, maintaining and evolving my entire earthly sojourn.

He said that the more peace I was able to access in my daily affairs, the greater service I would be performing for the entire planet.

Dr. Charlie was once asked by one of his colleagues — another psychologist with whom he was associated — how he managed to remain happy, buoyant and apparently patient with all the world all of the time. Dr. Charlie answered that he had made practicing the presence of peace the primary interest of his personal and professional life, and the single standard for all he did. He said it was easy, after a while, to remain peaceable when the practice of peace was consciously the most important thing in his life, ahead of all other concerns and possibilities.

He said that at the beginning of his studies in psychology he devoted all of his time to looking at and exploring all of the different things, thoughts and stories which excited his own sense of peace, of happiness, his own pleasure in living. He focused all of his efforts on associating with his own peace and discovered that the old wives tale, which suggests we can not go after or capture peace but that we must wait for it to come to us, was simply not true. He discovered, as already documented, that he was never able to practice the presence of peace while simultaneously thinking thoughts which troubled him, with which he was not at peace. He had learned that the most practical thing he could do was to put the practice of the presence of peace above all other interests in his life.

Dr. Charlie said that in his schooling he secretly vowed to accept only those concepts and teachings with which he was at peace, and to drop or ignore those teachings and concepts which he found troubling.

"I of course wanted to succeed in school," he said, "but I knew my practice of peace was even more important."

He said that by staying with this practice he quickly learned to be at peace with more and more concepts and diverse teachings and that the presence of peace eventually gave him both quick and uncommon insight into all areas of his professional discipline. He said that studying a subject without a peaceable state of mind was the least efficient, least effective or lasting approach, and only very rarely did it lead to even the slightest degree of practical application. Only after peace has been introduced and given its rightful priority does a subject come alive and useful for either the student or the teacher. This is why, again, he said, he has discovered the practice of peace to be the most practical, most true, most helpful and wise of all companions.

He said that he most often spent the first hours of his day simply writing down thoughts with which he was peace, sometimes on one topic in particular and other times on many different topics. Sometimes he would write down peaceable thoughts about the people and circumstances which he knew he would encounter in his day, or which he had already encountered on previous days. Sometimes he would write peaceable thoughts about world events and world leaders, or about community news or regional developments. He said he let the presence of peace itself lead him to address whatever topic was most appropriate for him at that moment. Sometimes it was personal and other times it was more communal or even planetary in focus. Sometimes, he said, he would take an entire book, which most often contained inspiring, peaceable sentences to begin with, and systematically uplift his thoughts by using the material of the book to invent new sentences with which he was even more at peace than the original sentences.

He said these early morning writing exercises helped initiate a pattern of thinking which remained with him throughout the day. To enhance this pattern, he said would often, prior to engaging a project or chore, rehearse a number of peaceable thoughts about the project, and then continue with the thoughts through the time it took to accomplish the project. After completion, he would often again pause to think back on the project and invent many new thoughts about that work that he found comforting and uplifting.

He said he would often engage the same process at night, before retiring, enveloping the near and far events and people of his day with peaceable thoughts. In this way, he said, he would spend his entire day thinking thoughts with which he was at peace, which inevitably led to the same process unfolding on the subtle planes in his dreams as he slept.

Dr. Charlie said he would often talk to Peace as if she was his mother, and they had a long and loving history. He would say such things as, "Mother, you have placed yourself here in my heart, and mind. When I forget your Presence, or ignore you, during my daily adventures, please remind me, nudge me back to wakefulness, for I want you first of all companions. You are much more important to me than any project or adventure or any of my brothers and sisters who may distract me. You have my permission, and my encouragement to catch my attention in whatever way you deem appropriate. I will come to you as often as I can. Please help me in fulfilling this desire."

"Of course I am with you always," Mother Peace might respond. "In whatever form you want me. I am pleased to remain your quiet and anonymous servant, or I am just as willing to beat the drums and clash the symbols, leading the circus parade. Most of the time you and I will just love each other like this, simply, peaceably, without fanfare or exaggeration. Your world is my world. My world is yours. We are in this together, forever. I am Mother, Father, sister, brother. I am the wind, the light, the birds in the trees, the grass beneath your feet. I am that which you seek. And I am that which propels you to seek."

Such conversations as this—and conversations even more sublime as well as conversations even more mundane—continued to unwind between Dr. Charlie and Mother Peace throughout the day. At times, however, there was simply no distinction between his own identity and the identity of Infinite Peace. At other times, there was no need to be expanded or engaged beyond his own ordinary personality, simply at peace with himself, doing common chores.

He said he naturally sometimes felt very light and sometimes felt heavier, like any other human being, yet he was no longer at war with these currents and had learned to consistently access his unvarying spirit, whether he was up or down. In this way he was never snarled in unhappiness or discouragement, though he did travel through such moods. On the whole he remained consistently in touch with peace, and devoted to this presence not only as an intellectual and spiritual discipline but also as simply and sweetly as a child is devoted to his mother or as a mother is devoted to her child.

"By training myself to consistently return to those thoughts which I am at peace," he said, "and consciously being at peace with thoughts which had previously caused me turmoil, I am now habituated to peace to such a depth and degree that it would be next to impossible for me to hold the habit at bay for any length of time. Indeed, I have no reason to do so, and the experience of peace is now as ordinary and fixed in my life as is tying my shoes and brushing my teeth."

Since Dr. Charlie had proven the ease and grace and naturalness of peace in his own life, for so many years, in so many different circumstances, he was naturally moved to share his methods and techniques with others. Yet his own ordinary enjoyment of peace, even more than his teaching and counseling, was the irresistible encouragement which others discovered in his presence. He was very ordinary, and at the same time extraordinary, in his peaceable consistency. Visitors and clients and friends felt immediately at ease, "at home" in his company, accessing their own peace as easily and consistently in his company as he himself was able to do. In the ordinary affairs of life he was extraordinarily easy to be with, whether in a restaurant, in a car, in his office, at home, or in larger gatherings. He was efficient, yet graceful and unhurried and able to make those around him appear equally efficient, equally graceful. He was practical, yet of the highest ideals, holding the highest views of himself and all mankind. His very presence brought a smile to the face of his friends and associates, and yet he was not a "star" or a superhero. The daily responsibilities which he attended to somehow seemed clean, simple, honorable. Yet they were also beautiful, elegant, profound. All of this was the result of his remaining with peace, inwardly and outwardly, as a matter of choice, of lifestyle and personal authenticity. In his presence one did not feel "obligated" or pressured to accept or share such a choice, such a lifestyle. Indeed, in his presence one felt more free and un-judged and more loved "as is" than with any other human being.

Dr. Charlie gave a very clear impression that my showing up in his presence was simply cause for more joy, more gratitude, awe and wonder. I did not have to "do" anything special to receive this response, or "be" someone in particular or noted, but rather I felt that my very *existence* elicited joy and peace from Dr. Charlie. Which, apparently, it did.

Even more extraordinary and comforting, it was quite clear that Dr. Charlie's peace did not *depend* on my presence, and was not, in fact, lessened by my departure. I simply shared his peace when I was with

80

him, and easily, spontaneously remembered, reconnected with my own peace during the sharing process. In this way, I discovered peace would remain with me for hours or days or even months after being in his company, such was his effect of returning me to that peaceable presence which is natural and common to every human being.

Dr. Charlie was as much at peace while filling out client records or vacuuming his office as he was while sailing or relaxing on a beach. He was naturally at peace while reading or when he was talking or when walking, whether alone or with friends. He was as much at peace while ironing as he was while watching football.

His lessons, his methods and techniques for accessing peace, are quite simple and easily learned, and yet could be continuously deepened, strengthened and improved over a lifetime.

"I am peace," he once confessed. "And that's enough. Peace has no opposite."

Having met Dr. Charlie, I feel I have reconnected with what has been with me since before the beginning of time. For that, I am deeply grateful.

First Letter:
Peace in Chartres and in Wal-Mart

My delightful Angelina!

How wonderful! Your first trip to "the continent"! I'm sure you'll have a delicious time — Great Britain, France, Italy! Wow! Send post cards, friend, (if that's what you enjoy to do!). I'll travel with you!

And since you asked (repeatedly begged!), I'll attempt to put on paper here for you a bit of what we have talked about in person. As you've already started to experience, when you actually take up these simple disciplines, your daily experience of peace becomes more and more consistent; your peace becomes more "ordinary," and more apparent. It also grows in depth and breadth. As you know, accessing peace *is* a conscious discipline, and not just a result or a by-product of something else you are doing. (*Am I at peace with these thoughts, yes or no. If the answer isn't an immediate and spontaneous yes, it's a no.*)

The "peace discipline" will serve you not only while you are in Europe but throughout your life, whether you be "at home or abroad." You'll discover that you enjoy peace while you are in the Chartres Cathedral or in your local Wal-Mart. Peace itself has no preference towards one or the other!

Before we dive in, let me assure you that my own peace does *not* depend on whether you yourself accept or practice these principles or methods while you're in Europe or when you're back home. Even though it is clear to me that you already *are* practicing these methods, after many years I've observed that my own awareness of peace remains almost always steady and self-sustaining, regardless of the acceptance or rejection of these discoveries by others. So you may continue to adopt all of these methods or decide to ignore them all or just take bits and pieces or even decide to revise them, and still I will remain deeply happy and at peace with you. (I can't help it!) You may pass these tools on or keep them to yourself. However you choose to respond to my sharing of these methods with you, my peaceable happiness with you is full. (I trust that this little confession frees you from any false sense of obligation that these words on paper might inadvertently elicit.) So let's get to it.

As you know, we are swamped with a flood of books and tapes offering to teach us to be happy, fulfilled, and thus, theoretically, at peace. These books are authored by self-help teachers, preachers, motivational speakers, sports stars and even political pundits who are quick to jump into the fray with advice on how to live a full and happy and peaceful life. You asked how I respond to them. Here's how: *I'm delighted with them, at peace with them, grateful for all of them!* (As you know, in my understanding, being peaceful and being grateful are two words for the same experience. If I'm not at peace with something or someone then I'm not being grateful. Without my peace, my words of gratitude may be politically correct, but they are completely hollow, and mean nothing.) So I confess I truly am at peace with this vast literature and the innumerable teachers of "full living." I honor it.

Here's why: As a lifelong student of peace, I've found that I can always (well, almost always) learn and enjoy something new about peace from everyone (almost everyone) who is brave enough to talk about it. Granted, what I learn and enjoy may not be what that person was hoping I'd learn, or believe I should learn. Still, I learn and enjoy what peace itself (herself) has to teach me in that moment. Peace is infinite. Peace uses all these people and products to express itself. Peace has no boundaries, no limits as to where It will express itself in the world. (As you know, I understand peace as a spiritual Presence, and thus the occasional Peaceful capitalizations! Don't expect me to be consistent with such play! Peace Herself really doesn't care!)

The point is that even politicians, lawyers and dour preachers who preach to us about a peace that they themselves may seldom experience have something new and sweet to teach us once we have trained ourselves to look behind their words. Peace is everywhere, and will peek out with a wink from behind the most somber of words and appearances.

The reason peace has an infinite number of "outlets" in the world is this: Peace is what the world is all about! Peace is the background screen upon which the movie drama of life is playing. When we pay attention first to peace, to the background screen, then everything else begins to make sense; life itself falls into place.

As we take up the disciplines that allow peace to show herself more regularly through our individual lives, we are taking the first step to bring harmony into our particular human affairs. By attending to the peace in our own lives — as a daily discipline — we are helping to bring an end to the wars, an end to injustice, an end to poverty. Becoming aware of and honoring our "background peace" is the most important thing (and most moral and most practical thing) we can do in life, for ourselves for all those around us. This is the "First Law of Peace." It's simple. When we are attentive to peace, we are serving life. When we are not attentive to peace, we are diminishing life. Our peace is our connection with the Divine. *"Peace First"* is a deeply lawful (though politically incorrect!) motto.

So my most basic and urgent encouragement is that you train yourself — which is in fact to simply *allow* yourself — to make your practice of peace the most important thing in your life. Your peace is your connection with the divine. So let your peace be the guide for all that you think, all that you do, all that you speak. As blasphemous as it may sound to some ears, I've discovered that our own attention to peace — which is also attention to our own inner joy — is the surest way we have to know and follow God's guidance for our lives. To love God means to be at peace with God. To love your neighbor means to be at peace with your neighbor.

Quibble over these equations if you want, but I'm an old guy. I speak from experience when I say that you can experience peace—which is to experience God—in every one of your relationships, in each of your activities, and while fulfilling all of your daily responsibilities. Such peace, although unusual, is in fact quite natural. It's how we were originally designed to live. (Kids do it all the time!) Would God want us to live in any other way than peaceful and happy?

Using the terminology from my religious background and professional training, I now recognize that the experience of peace and the experience of the Christ Consciousness and the experience of self-actualization and the experience of the Atman, the Buddha Mind, the Shekhinah, are all the same experience. Just the words are different. To love someone is to be at peace with that one. To be at peace with the person is how to serve that person. You have heard the scriptural injunction to give up all and follow Christ. My understanding of this is that we are each compassionately directed, invited, to give up all un-peaceable-ness and simply dwell with peace, which is our deepest self.

You can train yourself to engage your day life as if living in peace is your only moral option. You can understand that living in peace is a *moral choice* and that you can *choose* to make peace a regular response, and your daily companion. You are free to make the enjoyment of peace your primary career, your highest destiny, knowing that peace functions as a Vigilant Angel correcting, protecting and directing everything you do, at work, at play, at home or abroad.

As I've shared with you time and again, the principle is simple, if not easy. It's worth repeating: you enjoy your peace when you are at peace with the thoughts you are thinking. Whenever necessary, simply ask: *Am I at peace with this thought, yes or no?* If the answer isn't an immediate and spontaneous *yes* then it's a *no*. If the answer is yes—you are peace with your thoughts—that's perfect! Keep thinking them. If the answer is no, then you have two options:

a.) drop the thought with which you aren't at peace and find, or choose or create a thought with which you are more at peace; or

b.) choose to be at peace with the thought which a moment before you were not at peace.

I sometimes find it fun to pretend that I have an "inner thief" that I have to watch out for. When I'm not paying attention or being lazy about keeping my inner rooms, this "inner thief" steals the world's turmoil and pain and suffering, and brings it along with us in the form of thoughts and stories. When I suddenly wake up and see what this thief has brought home, I immediately feel guilty about stealing and keeping all this turmoil. I know these turmoil's are not mine. I know the inner thief picked them up, pretended they were ours, but I know they don't belong to me! So I just drop them. I don't try to remember where I stole them. I just drop the turmoil's, the thoughts and stories of pain and suffering. I walk away from them as soon as I realize I'm actually carrying stolen property. I know that turmoil does not truly belong to me. It was not my right, and certainly not my obligation to carry such things away. It's not my right or duty to carry turmoil any distance at all. Turmoil is not mine. When I realize I've stolen it again, I just drop it, and get away.

So—that's one game to play. Pretend there's a "turmoil thief" inside you. Be vigilant. Whenever you see that the little thief has picked up some turmoil, just drop it, right where you are. (Turmoil itself is the real thief, of course. It steals your life. So this is the game I sometimes play.)

Another game I play is to pretend that my peace is my bride. You can pretend peace is your groom. Since she is my bride, I enjoy to serve peace, nurture her, dote on her. (Of course, we're talking serving and nurturing and doting on the thoughts and stories with which we are at peace.) I pretend I as the groom and peace as my bride, are alone in our wedding chamber. I try to be attentive, watchful, tender with my peace. I give her room to breathe and grow. I dote on her. Do whatever she asks of me, and try to think of what she might ask even before she asks. Seeing peace as my bride, my lifelong companion, is a wonderful little secret game. She always loves to play it!

Another game I play with peace is to pretend I am a father providing a warm and safe place for my newborn infant—this peace child. You, of course, could pretend you are the mother attending to her newborn. Let your wonder, and your patience, unfold with this new presence in your life. Playing this game—that I am the parent of peace—I watch it grow and mature and get stronger, day after day. It's a wonderful game—to protect and serve and nourish peace. It's a life game that just gets better and better.

Enough about games. Let's just talk straight. Contrary to our previous training, we can simply *observe* that being at peace with all of our thoughts, and all of our feelings, all our stories is the most *practical* thing we can do in every circumstance, and in every relationship, even if we haven't yet perfected the process. Since being at peace is so practical, we can *decide* we're going to learn to be at peace with all that we see and hear and all that we don't see and don't hear. Such a decision about the deep, practical importance of peace in our lives is a powerful, life-blossoming decision. What we are at peace with and what we aren't at peace with does not need to be a random, arbitrary, misty, uncertain thing. We can *choose* to be at peace with more of our lives—*choose* to be at peace with more of our thoughts. Such a choice reveals the power and grace invisibly guiding our lives. But it's not magical. We can simply *choose* to be at peace with our ordinary thoughts, and the mundane stories we are already telling ourselves, or by choosing different thoughts and stories with which we are more comfortable, more at peace. If we aren't at peace with the thoughts and stories we are telling ourselves, let's just drop them, or decide not to fight them, to enjoy them, be at peace with them!

While you're in Europe, when you discover that you are not at peace with your thoughts, not at peace with what you see or hear, or what you don't see or don't hear, gently bring yourself again to the remembrance of the ever-available background presence of peace (Peace.) You can do this very easily, softly, by either releasing the thought you are thinking with which you aren't at peace or by deciding to be at peace with the thought which a moment before you were not at peace. Whichever of these is easiest for you to do in that moment, do that. The *method* to Peace is not the key. Peace Itself is the key. (And of course, when you come home from Europe, I encourage the same practice!)

As you've already experienced, there's great ease and comfort along with increased clarity and energy when we do this simple exercise—when we keep our inner rooms peaceable by releasing all that is unlike peace. When we discover that we have gone some time without an awareness of our peace—without thinking thoughts with which we are peace—we simply return to thoughts that we *are* at peace with, without feeling guilt or condemnation for our lapse. Rather than guilt or condemnation, we just enjoy our homecoming (like a bride to her groom!)

I find it helpful, and you might too, to set aside specific times, especially in the morning and in the evening, though other times during the day or at night work just as well, for meditation. Meditation can be very simple: just sit and enjoy thoughts with which you are at peace. That's all I do—I set aside some specific time to indulge myself with peaceable thoughts and stories. Or sometimes I'll engage in walking meditation, where I walk and consciously think thoughts with which I am at peace. Sometimes these thoughts take the form of prayer, or mantra. Other times, I find that reading helps me to think thoughts with which I am at peace, sometimes scripture, or scriptural studies, or other uplifting books. Other times I enjoy to journal—where I simply write one thought after another with which I am at peace, about whatever topic or person or idea I want to be more peaceful with. Such regular, concentrated "peace sessions" help me to bring depth and breadth to my ordinary day-life practice of peace.

Of course, the main "time" I practice enjoying my peace is while I am working, or commuting, or socializing, bathing, reading, eating, dreaming, sleeping. The main time is *all* the time! Whenever anything that is unlike peace presents itself to me, my practice is to quickly, gently return my thoughts, my feelings, my actions back to peace. I recognize that it is only peace itself that is able to dissolve the turmoil in the world. I've become a slave to peace, and have discovered that such slavery to peace has made me upright, and free and strong in the world, at ease with all I see and hear and think and feel. (I describe my practice, and its results, so that you too, if you are so inclined, might more quickly and expertly take up this delicious way of life, at home and abroad!)

To recognize that the most practical thing we can do in every circumstance and every relationship is a recognition that need not take years and years to dawn, although for many people it does indeed come late in their journey. With the aid of friends, and our work together, and your own inner vision, the central importance and practicality of peace can become as clear to you as the mid-day sun. I myself feel that peace is a fundamental aspect, or power of the divine. For me, peace is ceaseless, absolute, infinite and omnipresent, eternal. And although none of us yet practice peace to perfection, our imperfections are themselves perfect, when seen with through this peaceable light. (In other words, you can be at peace with both your perfections and your imperfections, and thus always peaceful!)

It is the character of peace itself — its light, its love, its freedom — that attracts us to its study and practice. Ceaseless peace was here before we came into our bodies and it will be here after we lay our bodies down. We have come from peace. We live now in peace. And we will return to peace. We ourselves — in our individual identities — did not create this peaceable condition, this joyful circumstance. In our individualized identities we are graced to simply abide with peace, more closely than bark abides with the tree. We are made out of it. The separation between ourselves and peace is only superficial, a surface appearance.

When we remember that enjoying our peace, practicing our peace is the first and most practical thing that we can do in any relationship or circumstance, then whatever else is happening in those relationships and circumstances will flow more easily, more naturally.

As I've mentioned, for me, remembering and practicing peace is my way to serve God, and my fellow human beings. For others, who doubt or simply don't believe in God, remembering and practicing peace is still a powerful way to serve life, and our fellow human beings. My experience shows that in such service we find our deepest freedom, and ease, our genius and our genuineness. When we focus on peace, when we remember peace — by focusing, remembering thoughts with which we are at peace — then turmoil and unhappiness naturally fade away. When we stand in peace, breathe, think and feel peace, all that we need is peaceably brought forth, and all that hinders us is peaceably removed, and who we are in our core is brought forth to the surface and nourished, and sent forth to nourish others. Such is the inner and outer power of peace.

But don't make this practice too hard. Don't worry if you're doing it right! The discipline of peace is both an art and a science that can be learned, adopted, matured, perfected, mastered, just like playing the piano. Such mastery, such perfection is not sudden. Still, as you learn and play even the earliest tunes, you discover a sweet delight. Peace, when practiced and matured, at last appears as perfectly ordinary, spontaneous, natural, ordained, which in fact it is.

So Angelina, let me remind you: Your peace is already with you, in you. Living with peace, in peace, is natural to you, as it is with everyone, though it is still somewhat rare for most folks to live this way. You do not need to create peace, or muster it up. It already abides in your heart, and has been there throughout all eternity. Peace is in all of our hearts, for we are all children of God, and this peace within is His (Her) sign to us.

If you are *not* enjoying your peace, it is *always* because of one simple reason: you are thinking thoughts with which you are not at peace. There is never another reason, inside or out. This is so simple, and yet so important, that I will repeat it: If you are not enjoying your peace, it is because you are thinking thoughts with which you are not at peace.

The delicious challenge that you have as you go off to Europe — and go off to the rest of your life — is to engage this simple experiment with your thoughts. Through this experiment — choosing thoughts with which you are at peace, dropping thoughts with which you aren't at peace, and being at peace with thoughts that previously caused you turmoil — you will spontaneously wake and live and move and have your being in peace, while in Europe, and while at the driver's license bureau. Taking up this discipline, you'll sleep and dream in peace. And then you'll wake again to ever deeper, ever more graceful peaceable-ness. Such is what has happened in my own life and by this very gentle, very simple practice you will discovers that it happens for you, too. In fact, the constant experience of peace is your inescapable *destiny*! (It is my joy to bring you this news!)

It is God's blessing, and His will that you companion with peace in this way, for He (She) *is* this ceaseless peace. Nothing that you or I have done in our individual lives has created this peaceable condition, this peaceable presence. Peace simply exists, and it is your right, and my right, our inheritance, to avail ourselves of it, constantly.

In spite of the volumes of books and tapes about living a full life, few of us are ever taught this basic, fundamental discipline for peace, nor are we reminded of it in our lives. But simple maturity requires that we now begin to practice this discipline, avail ourselves of this Presence, that we and the world might come into our rightful inheritance.

I am happy to be sharing these insights with you. I am happy for you, and with you. In our happiness, with our peace, we experience the same consciousness, the same being, the same life.

Until we are face to face again, sharing this peaceable life, our peace will remain our unbreakable bond.

In peace, dear Angelina, and bon *voyage*, with you —

(*Charlie*)

Second Letter:
Peace Waits Like a Faithful Servant

Hello Phil, old friend! —

It was great to be with you again. What a convention, eh? Such delightful encounters with old *compadres* are what make those types of stuffy gatherings worthwhile.

So okay: I promised I'd send you an outline of my own personal practice and its relation to this therapeutic profession we share. My own study has confirmed for me that my practices integrate and advance the more traditional, accepted therapies and techniques, but this is not, at least for me, the place to provide such documentation and cross referencing. Rather, I just want to continue our discussion on the transforming power of peace itself (Herself) and let the graduate students document as they see fit. I trust that what may turn out here to be a rather lengthy letter (I have a hard time holding back when I start talking about peace!) will help you with your presentation to

96

the Board and in making the changes there in the facility that you want to make (as well as in your presentation to the Universe, in making the changes you want to make!) I suspect my promise to write this letter (which I rarely do, these days) came about because of the wine, the warm evening, the laughter and pleasant company, but a promise is a promise. It's a delicious task. So without further ado...

As mentioned, I always suggest to my clients in our first session that bringing effortless peace into every relationship and circumstance is the most practical thing they can do, for themselves and for all those around them. And then I point out that the only way they can bring effortless peace into their relationships and circumstances is by being at peace with the thoughts they are thinking. I then guide them in the simple ways they might use to be more at peace with their thought stream.

Although I seldom mention it, such a basic observation of what's most practical (peace), and the techniques to magnify what's practical (e.g., being at peace with their thoughts), can be found in all of the world's scriptures, in all of the best psychoanalytic theorists, in the best of contemporary self-help and self-actualization literature. (My clients generally don't care about such. They just want to fine some peace in their lives and be happier!) If progress in our lives does not mean we are experiencing more peace, more happiness, who needs such progress?

At the convention, after my talk, another long-term therapist came up to me and said that in her experience a truly peaceful life was rare, and that it was a blessing, or talent, given only to a few. She also said that almost all those whom she would judge to be truly at peace had earlier in their lives experienced some sort of prolonged suffering, or deprivation or abusive relationships. She said she believed it was such early experiences that prompted the personal motivation toward finding peace, and the honoring of it as a worthy goal. She said her experience was that it took many years and much effort to overcome these early unhappy experiences and that without help—such as our own profession ideally affords—it is rarely accomplished.

I had no inclination to argue with the dear woman, or such a theory. My own clients, and the world at large, offer ample evidence of the prevalence of suffering and abuse, from early childhood to old age, and the heroic struggles many people make over many years to overcome such experiences. Nevertheless, my own experience of peace does not conform to this pattern, and I'm not convinced that others need follow it either. Further, I find that peace—and peaceable lives—to be quite prevalent, even ordinary, and easily documented, (though it has not in the past been politically correct in our profession to make such observations, or documentations. Thank God such a taboo is changing!)

As I mentioned over dinner, it did become clear to me at an early age that the experience of peace and the experience of God must be the same experience. Yes, the experience of God may be more than the experience of peace, but surely not less. So the experience of peace is a good place to start, and an easy standard to carry, in our spiritual walk.

From the moment I glimpsed the spiritual nature of peace, I have been unwilling to live for even an hour without at least a taste, or a glimpse of this inner presence. I am no more able to live an entire day without attending to the presence of peace than I am able to live a day without attending to air! I have made the practice of peace the focus of my life, and the focus of both my personal and professional practice. All the most influential world teachers, as far back as Socrates have pointed us to the necessity for peace in our daily lives. Although this is the case, seldom are we taught the practicality of practicing peace as a personal discipline.

It is my discipline, because it is what most interests me. So the presence of peace, as it reflects itself in my thinking, is what I pay attention to whether I'm eating or drinking or writing or cleaning or visiting with others. I have made peace the focus of my life, in waking and sleeping. I strive to resist (though I'm not always successful) the innumerable temptations to focus on anything unlike peace. My practice is to release all unhappiness, disown sorrow and regret. I feel they are unworthy of my attention, and unwelcome and unnecessary in my repertoire of responses. Scriptures and my own experience confirm that in my deepest heart I am at peace. Such a deep heart is all I need hold to.

In the early years of my discipline, I often tried to work on my problems — and/or my clients' problems — by bringing in the background presence of peace to the troubling thoughts and feelings and circumstances which arose. I would work with my clients, and on myself, to "clean up" our problems — find thoughts with which we were more at peace — so we could then more easily let go of the problems and simply get on about the day, enjoying whatever came up. I observed that in my own life I would often quickly tire of working on my problems and instead simply indulge myself with those thoughts which I enjoyed and was at peace in thinking, and finding thoughts that had previously troubled me that now I could be at peace with. I found this to be much more refreshing, rewarding and empowering than the "problem work" I had previously been engaging. Curiously, as I continued in this practice (of going directly to peace!), I found fewer and fewer problems arising, either within or without, and those that did arise were being resolved much more quickly, with much less effort than ever before. Naturally, I started guiding my clients in this same process — dropping the problems, going straight to peace.

I began living my life as though peace was always with me. In fact, I began pretending that I was peace itself, peace incarnate. It was not me, Charlie, living my life, but rather the presence of peace living its life through Charlie! With such an inner framework, where was I to escape to in order to consider troubles and unhappiness? I had no such escape. And I quickly learned to be a willing prisoner. I found that the presence of peace, living through me, took care of all my needs, all my histories, and all my future.

This is not to say, old friend, dear doctor, that various forms of unhappiness and turmoil did not present themselves. As you know, in our profession we daily open the door to a long parade of pour souls who have been taught to identify with unhappiness, express and magnify their troubles. And even without such clients, in my own life all manner of real and illusory pains and discomforts arose, mental, emotional and physical. And such suffering appeared not only in me but also in those I loved most in the world. Worries and hurts from the past revisited me and anxieties and doubts about the future often claimed my attention. Welcome to life on earth! I'm a human with human experiences just like everyone else.

I was perhaps even more alert to these turmoils in my life than others might be, and suffered more acutely because I had consciously determined to make the presence of peace my constant companion, my life's work, my faith, my refuge. Therefore to be forced to continue to wrestle with all that unhappiness seemed to mock my philosophical position, make me look (and feel!) ridiculous for the entire world to see.

During these times my understanding and conviction about the practicality of peace did not waver. Rather, I was frustrated with my own wavering devotion to it. Had I been more mature in my practice of the presence of peace during this time I have no doubt that I could have allowed peace itself to gracefully work its healing ways. It was my own stubborn clinging to the pains and sorrows, fears and frustrations of my prodigal mind that caused or at least magnified and prolonged the troubles in my life. At one point I was even troubled by my first hand experience that simply being at peace appeared to be so easy, so simple and natural and not the long and difficult process which our profession demanded it to be.

At this time in my life I knew in my heart that peace was both the "background screen" and the fundamental building block of everything in the universe, both subtle and gross. So it was a mystery to me why I—along with my clients and the world at large—continued to experience the duality of both war and peace, happiness and unhappiness. I could not resolve this duality. I finally decided that I would no longer try to explain it away and instead decided to simply be at peace with both the wars and the peace, the happiness and the unhappiness that came into my life. I gave up the fight. I did not want to fight the one in favor of the other any longer. I had faith in my understanding of peace, and thus determined to be at peace, as best I knew how, with the pain and sorrow, the fear, grief, and suffering in the world. I felt very much alone in conducting this experiment (being secretly at peace with all that arises), since everybody in the world naturally resists suffering and war and unhappiness. Why wouldn't we?

However, having made this decision, and put it into practice as best I could, I discovered that all my little wars—my pains, fears, sorrow, doubts—began to dissolve, leaving me to enjoy the presence of peace without interruption. I discovered that this peaceable presence was, indeed, in the deep center of my heart, and that if I simply stood back it flowed from there to encompass the world. All that was unlike peace was washed away by this inner stream. Once I finally recognized and honored the centrality of the presence of peace in my life, the world's pain, sorrow and affliction never again found a central place in my awareness. Such suffering was still obvious, of course, but it was consigned to a peripheral, non-engaged, non-empowered locale.

As I mentioned to you at the conference, this decision to be at peace (in my thoughts, if not with my actions) with both pleasant and unpleasant circumstances was a decision I arrived at some years ago. Since that time I have experienced increasing peace, simplicity and contentment. My daily discipline is to be at peace with my own thinking, and thus be at peace, as best I can, with everything I do, and everything I say and in every relationship that arises, and not to do anything or say anything or think anything with which I am not at peace. (This practice also leads me to be at peace with everything I don't do, don't say and don't think!) Following this discipline, I give the presence of peace every opportunity to guide me, correct and strengthen me in my daily activities. This peaceable presence has become my wise, gentle yet very powerful companion and friend.

As politically incorrect as it may sound, I confess to you that my daily condition now is simply this: happiness and peace, from morning until night, and into my dreams. I have no confusion or hesitancy about my work or my leisure or any of my daily activities—I follow peace, am prompted by peace, and I move with peace. It's a sweet, pleasant empowered way of living.

Over time I have discovered that I have abandoned most of the language and ritual and trappings of both my professional and religious life. The trappings that remain are those that arise spontaneously in me as the result of attending to peace, to happiness. In both business and leisure, in duty and idleness, my only intent is to deepen my awareness of the presence of peace. I sometimes talk to the peace presence and I sometimes talk *for* this presence. I habitually wait for the peaceable presence to talk to me, and for me and through me.

This practice, or more specifically the state of consciousness that this practice leads to, is not a state that is easily kept secret from others. I have ceased trying. I neither exaggerate nor dim my peaceable state. The presence of peace moves me sometimes into deep rapture and at other times into tickled delight and other times into childlike wonder, or mature contentment, each in its own appropriate time and place. Most often it is a simple, willing contentment and pleasure in the moment's artistry. I am the servant, as well as lover of peace, locked in a lifetime contract.

I am assuming that this is what God wants from us, for us. (If not, then who needs such a God!) In different terms, I consider peace to be my employer, (Employer) as well as my spouse (Spouse) with whom I have an unbreakable bond. I am no longer tempted to stray from peace, either as my employer or my spouse. More precisely, the temptation to stray is there, (the world's suffering continues!) but its persuasive power has dimmed. The frustrations, sufferings and turmoil that arise in me, and around me—these temptations toward a different employer for my thought—do not any more move me from my work, my devotion. I sometimes discuss these temptations with my employer (peace), my mate (peace), and together we arrive at wisdom, most often accompanied with humor and delight, as to their proper dispatch.

At other times I do not bother my Loved One with these trifles, and on my own dismiss them quickly. And yet, even then I know my Loved One is with me, aware of my service, cognizant of the work, the devotions I perform. The presence of peace is a full-time companion, a 24-hour employment, and for this I am eternally grateful. My loved One—this Peaceable Presence—feeds me and clothes me and houses me and brings me all the wonders of the world. Yet, even without food or clothing or housing or pleasures I would remain with the ceaseless presence of peace, asking nothing else but her company. She is my only need, my only want, my only desire. (Forgive me, old friend, for waxing poetic, falling into mystical swoon. It is one of the reasons I do not write much about my Beloved. Words quickly carry me away!)

The practice of the presence of peace is simple and natural. Alas, due to faulty education many people have, for example, eaten or sexed or traveled to great excess year after year and have still not experienced the continued peace (Peace) which is their birthright. Many who live in the finest suburban McMansions, or the House on the Hill or who drive leather-seated Lexus SUV's and wear Tommy Hilfinger's custom threads have not yet claimed the simple, prolonged joy and peace for which they yearn. Likewise, many of those at the top of our corporate infrastructure, or in the Hollywood royalty with annual incomes in seven or eight figures do not yet awaken in the morning with the precious gratitude for life that spontaneously arises from this practice I share.

Speaking of sharing, peace and I have a thousand secrets, as do all spouses and employers. Yet it is our intent to share all we have, as I do now with you. We withhold nothing, give as much as any are willing and able to take from us, for our store is inexhaustible. Our relationship is tender, sweet, secret, deep, yet also raucous, tangy open and swift. We are all things to each other, and nothing—nothing, nothing, nothing—is lacking! This is how it is with my spouse (Spouse), my employer (Employer), this peace (Peace) I am pointing you towards, already residing there within you.

So again, what is the practice? As we discussed at the convention, my most common practice is to simply remember that peace is in fact present and that is my natural state of being and that anything unlike peace that I am experiencing within or without is unnecessary and indeed, unnatural. I know that the infinitely peaceable presence is always present with me and thus I permit myself to again and again turn my attention to it, as naturally as the rain falls to earth or as rivers rush to the sea. I allow both my future and my past— thoughts about my future and past—to be absorbed by peace. When I think of the future I think only of further peace and when I think of the past I think only of past peace. I know that many people—and especially those in our "helping profession"—might consider such a way of thinking to be narrow and unrealistic. Nevertheless, I have discovered this way of thinking to be the key to expanded consciousness and empowered being. Such a way of thinking is what makes—or brings—heaven to earth.

Using this discipline of thought, I am submerged from morning to night in the joy of being. Others who practice the same discipline report the same thing. I have found such submersion to be both efficient and practical in conducting my daily affairs. To others I appear quite ordinary (which I am.) Indeed, *exceptionally* ordinary, and thus non-threatening and easy to be with. Only when I stray from this discipline do my daily affairs become tangled and somewhat chaotic and only when I neglect the presence of peace do I sometimes appear threatening or aloof or hard to get along with. I have discovered that being submerged in peace is the most practical and harmonious way to live an ordinary life!

I have no doubt that what I am doing in giving my attention to the infinitely peaceable presence is not extraordinary. In fact, it's quite ordinary, natural, the way we were meant to live. Granted, in our time and culture and in our educational systems we do not ordinarily articulate the ordinary human being's fundamental affinity for peace. Still, I posit that it is the most common and desirable and healthy of all human obsessions, and thus deserving to be made overt and intentional. I am sure that the discipline of the practice of the presence of peace is the very force, the essence, of evolutionary advancement.

Of course, some would contend that prayer and meditation are what connect us with the force of evolutionary advancement. I would agree. I do devote time in both morning and evening to prayer and meditation. Yet my practice in "formal" prayer and meditation is no different than my practices throughout the day, when I'm playing, working or engaged in social activity. I turn to the presence of peace to guide my thinking, toward what I enjoy and away from that which I don't enjoy. (As mentioned previously, I assume we might all agree that joy and peace are two words for the same presence, and that they are both qualities of the nature of God. If God is not Joyful, not Peaceful, why would anyone stoop to serve such a Force?) As I attend to the presence of peace, I attend to the divine.

Although in my prayer and meditation I often engage traditional forms from the various spiritual traditions, I do not feel confined or obligated by such forms, and am ready and able to follow my own peaceable impulses in creating new forms. For example, in my meditations I have at times enjoyed to envision myself in the form of a cloud of peace, moved through the peaceable sky by winds of peace, above a continent of peace, beneath a galaxy of peace. I experience myself releasing rains of peace, which in turn circulates back up from and to peace. As you might guess, I find such playful meditations useful to clear the inner atmosphere!

In other, more mechanical meditations, I might envision myself as an automobile, fueled by peace, fired by peace, driven by peace, on tires of peace towards a peaceable destination along a peaceful highway, coming from and going to a peaceable garage.

How silly, of course! And yet I find such peace focused meditations often buoy my day — (while driving in the rain for instance!) — and they are no less unrealistic, in my view than prayers and meditations where I envision myself as an troubled man with a troubled past, unpleasant present and a shaky future that I hope to manipulate through prayer or meditation. In my experience the peace of the moment can and does reveal itself through all forms. I understand the material universe itself to be only a small speck residing in a vast ocean of peace. Thus, as I identify myself with the presence of peace, all forms are me, are mine. The universe is mine to play in and with. Isn't this what God created it for?

Yet the play of peace goes even further. At times the presence of peace takes me out of form all together, to that timeless, spaceless (worldless and wordless!) Virgin Quiet, Vibration-less Bliss which is uninterrupted by the imploding and exploding of galaxies. My body remains in form while my Self encompasses the cosmos. It is a simple, sweet, contented state that Mothers all that arises. I know that in some traditions such a mystical state is viewed as rare, holy, blessed, the highest attainment of unique saints and seers. Yet I confess to you it is not—it is in fact quite accessible to all, not far off, the natural unfolding of a peaceful mind.

Others, of course, call this state delusional, without substance or empirical proof, socially irresponsible and bereft of productive engagements. It's true that in such a state all is complete and in need of no correction. It's also true that in such a state social bonds dissolve their hold and no longer motivate the peaceably contented one.

Nevertheless, my experience shows that a tenderness arises from seeing the cosmos thus, and the bonds between the seer and the seen are filled with light and love and trust. If such a tenderness is delusional I would contend that it is a divinely drawn delusion, much keener, more useful and serviceable than the delusions of the world where "reality" leads us to commit unspeakable mayhem, treachery, deceit. Alive in peace I find no need to trespass against my neighbor, nor to run from what others might see as unpleasant chores, nor to extend myself ahead of others to attain some imagined gain. My peace remains complete, sufficient to every purpose, and threatened by none. If this is delusional, I happily accept it, live within it, have no inclination to dissolve it. Yet I am convinced that such a state is the natural state, the ordinary state, the truth of being. Every day that I practice peace my mind grows cleaner, my heart more tender, my work more sure and my rest much deeper, my leisure more playful.

I know that it is the presence of peace (Peace) Herself, working within me and outside me that has brought me to this discipline, this way of living and this view of both the cosmos and my own back porch. If my view is to change I will happily leave it up to this same peaceful force to make the changes. (And if such changes should be offered through *your* response to these methods that I share here, then I am eager to hear from you. And if you enjoy these words and these methods – or have different takes, different views – then I would happy to hear that, too. Regardless of your response to this letter, I do find great peace in this professional and brotherly bond that we have.)

Time to get back to more local work responsibilities. (A letter such as this is not work for me – but rather pure indulgence!) So I'll release you now to return to your own daily framework of peace, as I return to mine. Say hello and give a hug to Alice, and the children. Until we share again our peaceable musings, I remain –

Your Peaceable Friend –

(Charlie)

Third Letter:
God Did Not Lead You to These Troubles

Hello Julie,

As usual, it was nice to be with you again. In regards to your questions about Dr. Jackson and his affairs, and your own place in them, let me assure you again that harmony is present. Not in the future, not in the past, but right now. Let me encourage you to put your attention on the present harmony, and let Dr. J. and all his troubles be lifted by your quiet concern.

If you'll permit me the big picture, my understanding is that the invisible principle of peace, from which the universe comes forth, is also Intelligence Itself. This Peaceable Intelligence is aware of the minute needs and eternal potentials of Its every creation, Its every manifestation, including you and me, and Dr. J. We can train ourselves to relax into this Intelligence, this Peace, and let it (It) do its own work.

As you know, in the old traditions we are told to love God, and then warned of the terrible damnations which we will suffer if we refuse, or forget or neglect to love Him. In this new tradition, we are encouraged to love the presence of peace (Peace). All we need do is participate in the unfolding of peace, acknowledge and magnify peace, within and without. Refusing to do so does not bring the vengeance of peace. Indeed, peace itself works to seep through our refusal, to get around, and inside our refusal, to awaken us to the ease, beauty and simplicity with which She (peace) works to fill our lives. The peaceable presence wants to surprise us with Her charms, Her fullness, Her willing and eager availability. When we expect Her, She is there. When we don't expect Her, still, She is there!

We are never far from this presence. It is our inner reality. In the greatest tragedy, the greatest despair, the deepest darkness, the peaceable presence waits like a faithful servant, a magical friend able to immediately retrieve whatever we need to help dissolve or at least ease our distress. It is peace itself that gives us patience, forbearance, fortitude, courage to meet and conquer every unhappiness which would test our faith. And the presence of peace makes us eager to move on, to abandon distress, to resolve our difficulties, that we might quickly resume our native state—which is peace itself with its natural buoyancy. (So no, you need not drown in Dr. J.'s storm of troubles. Cling to your inner life raft!)

Unlike the false theology of the old traditions, we need never assume that God has lead us into unhappiness, nor does God need or use unhappiness to solidify His place in our lives. The divine peaceable presence is complete, sufficient, without an opposite.

113

Peace needs only peace to express its nature, its presence (Presence,) its purpose. There is no need, or place, anywhere in the universe for unhappiness. Peace Itself is All, Perfect, Absolute, Unchallenged. And in this we rest. (e.g., the presence of peace — or God — did *not* lead you to these troubles with Dr. J. to test you!)

The good news is that in the face of troubles, peace engenders bravery and persistence. We might see that Dr. J. is relying on his worldly success — his promotions and transfers and victory over colleagues, you included — in an effort to find and secure his peace. Forgive him. It's the way we were all trained, and encouraged. It's a long road, however, and seldom does the traveler ever arrive. Be clear, though: peace itself is not opposed to or in conflict with worldly success. Indeed, peace is the root and life force of such success. Yet worldly success is not the *cause* of peace, nor can worldly success ever give but a fleeting taste of a meat which is meant to be chewed continually.

My understanding is that the experience of peace is in fact so natural, so native to us, that in our youth we often overlook its presence and assume we can magnify its radiance by further accumulations of people, things, and positions. As you know, Dr. J. has recently experienced set-backs in his worldly affairs, and such experiences have caused him temporary confusion and discontent. Such occurrences in mood and outlook will continue until he (and we and the rest of the world!) discover that peace is based on nothing but itself — has no cause outside its own infinitely beautiful presence. All things, people, positions and events come and go, yet peace remains, as surely as the cradle of the universe remains to gently uphold and give space to the swirling galaxies.

I have absolutely no doubt that the presence of peace accompanies Dr. J. wherever he goes, wherever he is, regardless of the mood or outlook with which he dresses his momentary thoughts and feelings. If Dr. J. should choose to acknowledge the already existing Presence of Peace, and to consult this inner presence about the major and minor events of his day, he will discover peace immediately there. It will bring the rose back to his cheeks, and lightness to his step. Regardless of his outer worldly circumstances, he will immediately experience a return of the buoyant mood that accompanied his former professional success. This is not a magical undertaking—this consulting with the presence of peace. It is quick, direct, easy.

We often mistakenly assume that such dark and deep and heavy moods, as Dr. J. is exhibiting, require prolonged and intensive care before they dissolve. In fact, a mere glimpse of the presence of peace is sufficient, because an inch of peace dissolves a mile of grief. And anyone, regardless of circumstance, regardless of the depth of despair into which he has fallen, retains the capacity to allow a single inch of peace to penetrate the moment's world.

The simple act of remembering the Presence of Peace is sufficient to activate Its power, no matter the circumstance, even in the face of death itself, and surely when presented with the demise of worldly hopes, relationships or expectations, or pleasant conditions. A glimpse of the pre-existing peace behind all form aligns all outer circumstances with the deep harmony of life. Such a glimpse of peace releases wisdom in us, which moves us to act spontaneously with grace, swiftly and precisely in meeting whatever the momentary conditions demand. Peace gives us courage, strength and insight, and thus is our greatest ally in all life's challenging moments.

So my encouragement to both you (and Dr. J., should he ask) is to return your attention again and again to the simple truth of the presence of peace within you. You do not, to begin, require the blazing sun of Absolute Bliss, but rather a single beam of gladness, about the simplest thing, the smallest thing. When you have found this single beam, just remain with it. You'll soon discover yet another grain of peace appearing, and then another. Let peace into your life through the silliest excuse, the most insignificant occurrence. You need not exaggerate it. Let it be just a tiny grain, a single inch (or half inch!) of peace. But keep your attention on it.

This suggestion to rest your attention again and again on whatever in the universe provides you with even a spark, or a glimmer of peace has its ulterior motive, for wherever such spark, such glimmer appears, there is the Infinite Presence of God.

You'll discover that this exercise—of bringing your attention again and again to specks and glimmers of peace—such an exercise grows over the weeks, months and years. Through such practice you will build a foundation which can not be undone (by even the most powerful of colleagues, lovers, family or friends). This practice of the presence of peace builds a foundation of stone, made to last 10,000 years. It is on this foundation that a rich, beautiful, generous life is built.

Such an exercise — (as we've shared, at length: simply turning your attention to peace, being at peace with the thoughts you think, dropping or reframing the thoughts with which you are not at peace) — such an exercise goes unnoticed, at first, and is often inadvertently challenged by the words and moods and outlook of many of our slumbering peers. Yet over time such practice builds up again all the successes, and more, which youthful folly gained and lost. In maturity we gain the wisdom that the true goal — peace — was here present all along. Returning thought again and again to peaceable appearances is continual prayer and thanksgiving.

Dr. (J.) will discover these truths as surely as a householder would discover, sooner or later, an intruder in his bed. It is not your work to change him. You work is not to bang him over the head with what is here presented, but rather enjoy him and be at peace with him and his ways, and let your peace communicate with his peace to present whatever lessons might most appropriately be offered in that particular moment. As you recognize the presence of peace in him, you are his friend, companion and helpmate. The more peace you see, the more helpful you are. Sometimes such vision is communicated in words, but peace itself (Itself) requires only itself, and so sometimes the simple vision is sufficient to effect the cure.

You need not trouble yourself overly much with the affairs of Dr. (J.) In fact, the more you are at peace with him in his troubles, or in spite of his troubles, the less hold they have on him, and you. If you can not think of him without despair, it is best to not think of him at all. It is even better, though, to think of him with all your peace, for such thoughts are helpmates to him and this is the right and proper regard for friends and colleagues.

And it is with such peace that I think of you, dear lady, who, out of your own concern for the peace of others, has brought this matter to me.

In peace I remain affectionately yours, and the galaxies can not part us!

(....*Charlie*)

Fourth Letter:
Are You at Peace with Your Thinking?

Hello again, Mrs. Olinksy,

Your delightful niece Alicia encouraged me to write to you. It was nice to be with you both. Alicia said you were very much moved by our conversation (as was I!) and that you had begged her to find out more about this peaceable way of life I teach. I suspect you are already living this life, in your own way. So I'm happy to share with you a little more here about how I do it, and the benefits and enlightenments which have been showered on me because of this habit of continually placing attention on the presence of peaceyes. May your joy in receiving this little missive be as great as my joy in writing it (?).

As I mentioned in our brief meeting together, it is my inner discipline to keep my attention on the presence of peace as much and as often as I am able. The discipline itself is actually quite simple to explain, though in the beginning not necessarily easy to master. The discipline is to simply inquire whether you are at peace with your thinking, and if you're not, either drop what you're thinking or choose to be at peace with it. Don't hold on (?) to thoughts with which you are not at peace. Don't talk about or say anything you are not at peace in saying. This naturally leads to not doing anything you are not at peace to do. The principle is simple: You are at peace when you are peace with the thoughts you are thinking.

Following this principle, I am training myself not to tell myself or anyone else troubling or upsetting or unhappy stories about people, places or events with which I myself am not at peace. My reason for this practice is founded on my perception that peace is a sign of the Presence of God, the Divine Spirit. I understand my devotion to the presence of peace to be the most natural, most obvious, most sacred activity I am able to perform. I intuit that peace is a Presence available throughout the universe. So peace itself is not broadened by my attention to it, but I am broadened, I am more myself, and am more in the world, in my right place as my attention goes to and rests in this presence of peace. I have come to understand that peaceable presence is the original source, the starting place of my attention.

I have now come to a point in my life where this presence is my constant companion, my very breath, my thought, my feeling, word and deed. The Presence of Peace (I sometimes capitalize these words, because they are signatures of the Divine) continually feeds me with new sights and sounds and thoughts and feelings with which to more fully enjoy Her Presence. There was a time in my life when I thought surely I would burst with happiness, and I struggled to dampen the flow, so that those around me might not notice. At last I did indeed burst, and all my efforts to dampen my peace, my happiness were abandoned. My relations with others are now simply one more way to relate to Peace Herself. Peace and I are alone in the universe, and often I myself am not here.

Confessing this, I must also quickly admit that my discipline—my journey in peace—is not yet finished, not yet mature. Like everyone else, I get bummed out, unhappy at times. However, because of my long time training along this path it seems to be Peace Herself who sounds the signal to bring me back when I forget Her. I return to Peace as if awakening from an unintended nap, or a thoughtless distraction. Such straying from peace generally occurs when I am paying attention to the suggested selfishness, shortcomings or insensitivity of others, near or far, and more particularly how such selfishness or insensitivity of others adversely affects me. My own experience confirms that the only adverse effect others can have on me is when I allow their actions, words or posture in the world to generate thoughts in me with which I am not at peace. Or more precisely, when I *hold on* to and magnify the thoughts that they generate with which I am not at peace. (The presence of peace is always with me, just as the presence of peace is always with you. Sometimes we forget or ignore this presence!)

I have learned that the only way I am able to help others who are suffering or conflicted is by remembering the natural supremacy of peace, in me and in them. Peace has the power to dissolve all that is unlike itself!

When you make practicing the presence of peace your life discipline—a discipline which I intuit you have already adopted, to a degree—you discover that when you forget it or ignore it for whatever reason you can always quickly return to it, because peace itself is in fact never absent. As I said, it is a presence throughout the universe. This happiness can fall behind the clouds of thoughts and feelings that we do not enjoy, but such thoughts and feelings have no real root. The simple process that always works to restore peace is to either chose to be at peace with the thought which a moment before we were not at peace or choose to put our attention on something or someone which *is* more easily enjoyed, with which we are more at peace. Above the clouds of all our daily drama and worry and unhappy speculation, peace, like the sun, keeps on shining. Our work, day after day, is to see through the clouds.

To do so, I confess that I sometimes play a game where I imagine peace has come to earth and assumed the form of my invisible companion. Playing this game, I talk with peace, or let peace talk with me. For example, this morning in the grocery store I found myself thinking, "Thank you, Peace, for waiting here with me in this long, slow moving line, behind this impatient, foul-mouthed young businessman who wants my agreement with his frustration." (My thought in the store went much quicker than it took me just now to write it out!)

Peace quietly responded, "Where else could I be? And thank you for remembering me, and let's thank this fellow for prompting us to get back together!"

Curiously, at that moment, before I had a chance to say a word to the young guy, who had been complaining to me about the wait, two more cashiers showed up and the young fellow was moved first in line with his purchases. I grinned big.

In just this way, I have discovered that it does not require much contact, long discourses or repeated efforts for the Presence of Peace to reveal Herself. She is willing and eager to be here with me—and those around me—at the slightest opening, the most timid of invitations. In Her Presence I feel a grin spread spontaneously across my face, and a clearing of clouds in my mind, and a peaceable-ness in my heart. I confess that after many years of practice such a condition is now my most common daily experience, the most ordinary "state" in which my life is lived. I do not consider this state to be extraordinary or heroic. Peace is very simple, very obvious. I am confounded why anyone would choose to ignore it, or to live as if it were not immediately and consistently available. In my understanding such a choice—the choice to ignore the presence of peace—arises from our faulty educational and cultural momentum, and not from the fundamental reality, the Peaceful Nature of Being.

With the presence of peace as my constant companion, I am no longer nervously seeking it in my outer affairs or in sensory stimulations. I am at peace with what arises and am content with what does not arise. I am keenly involved with daily activities—for the presence of peace frees me from doubts and reservations—yet I require no residuals, no paybacks from these activities because payment is made in full— my peace is complete—at the time my actions are performed.

In truth, I recognize that everyone is likewise in the presence of peace, is likewise already complete and content in their natural condition, though awareness of this natural condition of peace is not yet widespread. The peace which is ours for the asking in every moment, most people accept only fleetingly, tentatively, without trust or faith. Peace is the nature of the Divine and is thus everywhere and always urging Itself into new form, tender offerings, consistent confirmations. When I turn my attention to the presence of peace, which is very practical, reasonable and fair, I am immediately rewarded and confirmed on my path. Turning to peace, waking to peace, the presence of heaven on earth reveals Itself, and that which was mundane and bothersome reveals its beautiful utility. I daily train myself, stretch myself to receive more and more of these peaceable perceptions. Knowing that peace is ever-present, I prove it more and more. I recognize the current of peace which flows through my mind and heart and physical body, and I no longer fight to suppress it, disassociate from it or reinterpret it. I release it to its own natural end, and discover the world grows lighter because of it.

When I make the practice of the presence of peace the highest priority in my life, I discover it is ever more accessible, and quick to fulfill the faith I have placed in it. I more and more intuit that nothing can prevent the tender ministrations of peace, yet by my darkened thoughts and wandering attention I sometimes ignore these peaceable pamperings, and blind myself to their signals.

I am more and more learning to relax into peace, follow its gentle promptings, accept its quiet attendance. As peace fills my thought it likewise fills my past and future and the nature of eternity comes clear. In peace, the body is constantly refreshed and does not grow old. I move from peace into peace and time itself is cradled with Her unmoving Hands.

These same Hands likewise cradle my daily individuality. I now know that the presence of peace is the basis and power of all individuality. As I open my inner doors to the gentle rising of peace, the outer pressures of my day-life fall away (and I spontaneously meet such pressures more precisely and more artfully!) The taste of nectar, falling from within, becomes apparent, no matter my outer circumstance. I experience a perfect delight in completing my daily affairs. The blossoming of consciousness, while pumping gas or watering the lawn, is unmistakable.

As I said, in our brief conversation together I recognized this same awakening occurring in you. In your own way, you, too, have been in training, preparing for the blossoming. (It is why I agreed to write this letter!) I share your wonder and gratitude. We have seen the priority of peace, and have honored it. We will naturally continue to deepen and broaden this peaceful state, because once exposed to such an eternal presence we are never satisfied with anything less. The peace we know can not be taken from us. Once the doors have opened, and the rooms expanded to let in light, the peace itself refuses contraction. We move, in waking and dreaming, in work and at play, at rest and in motion, in quiet and in talking, with the current of peace running through our mind, like the sailor, his hand on the rudder, sure of his direction, regardless of the wind's wide shifts.

In scriptures we are told of the story of Jesus and the disciples crossing the sea, with Jesus asleep when a storm arises. The frightened disciples awaken the Master and with a word from Him the storm is calmed. Jesus gently chided them for being so troubled about such things. In truth, it is not our peace that sleeps but our awareness of peace, our attention to peace that is so often dormant. Jesus recognized that He and the Father were One-- He and the Christ were One. Thus Jesus was Himself peace incarnate. It is this peace -- this Christ-- that teaches us, saves us, redeems us still.

I share my discoveries here about the nature of the presence of peace that resides in each of us, a peace which is one with Spirit, Love, Godliness-- I share these discoveries only that you might find in my words confirmation and support for your own peace, and that you might quicken and embolden your own adventures with peace. Due to our faulty education and cultural slumber we are sometimes tempted to forget the innate presence of peace. So to share with each other and remind each other of these basic blessings is not impolitic. The peace which I have come to know in all of my hours is not due to a unique capacity in me, but rather to my consistent elevating, prioritizing of the presence of peace as the most practical presence to look for in every relationship and every circumstance. This is the most practical thing I can do both for myself and for those around me, and for any who, even at a distance, might for one reason or another contact my consciousness. To let my thoughts be guided by peace is my first service, my basic act of gratitude which I offer to my time and place on earth. From this first service-- this first peace -- all other services arise.

Yet even were there no other humans alive, nor even earth itself, or this solar system or this galaxy, still, I would fill this consciousness, my consciousness with peace. Such peace is the primal presence, the first life, God's Mood. To have this primal consciousness and the added delight of morning bird song, cool breeze and happy companions is a grace and beauty beyond belief.

I am easily at peace with all my thoughts and feelings about you, and your work and your relations with your world. I will continue with such thoughts, such feelings until there is no thought or feeling anywhere in the universe.

I remain, yours, In Peace —

(*Charlie*)

Fifth Letter:
Peace Itself Is the Guide

Hi Bob —

I trust the Coast is treating you well and that you spend your days lazing on the beach. I smell the sweet salt air!

I've received several letters this week from Grace DuChamps. Once again she is asking for more guidance with the peace practice. Apparently, it was your encouraging that led her to write. Because of her circumstances, she asked that I communicate back with her through you.

As you know, at some point in her life she will discover that it is the presence of peace itself, ever close at hand, that will most effectively, tenderly and immediately guide her, instruct her, once she recognizes its voice, already speaking in her day. Nevertheless, it is our destiny, and great pleasure to be instruments of peace, and share what we have learned of the ever-deepening presence of bliss. Clearly (perhaps because of you!) she has faith in my instructions, and so my first instruction is for her to turn her eyes, and her faith to the presence of peace within her own awareness, even if she can glimpse, in this troubled season, only a sliver of the stuff. As you know, you and I are but the outer reflection of what it already present within her. We are now here for her only because peace was first present within her! Our reflections for her of peace will of necessity come and go, but she has continual access (by divine right!) to the joyful presence which abides within her. This is always the first lesson: the peaceable presence is already residing inside each of us, and is only reflected outwardly.

Devotion to this presence of peace is akin to devotion to a spouse, or to children, or to parents or to a great cause or worthy work. Yet devotion to peace must precede devotion to all these other devotions, even our devotions to family or church or synagogue, because without peace our devotions have no balance, no art, no nourishing energy.

Learning to live with the awareness of peace, in the presence of peace, with peace as a first and constant companion, is the secret to a fruitful, productive and generous life. Practicing this presence is practicing the highest human activity, and through such practice all the world is uplifted, and the practitioner himself, herself, fulfills the demands of destiny. (How mysterious, that we can say here in a single paragraph — this upon which entire lifetimes depend!)

The true practice of peace begins with the fundamental insight that such practice — the practice of peace — is the most important, most practical and most prosperous thing we can do. The practice is more important even than meeting work deadlines or schedule completions. The practice is more important than attending to family responsibilities or even religious obligations. The practice is based on the insight that from the presence of peace—from the moment by moment awareness of this presence—all other blessings flow, and all other obligations are met. The scriptures suggest, "Seek ye first the kingdom of heaven and all else will be added unto you." If the kingdom of heaven is not *at least* a basic consciousness of peace, who needs heaven! So let's develop this basic consciousness of peace, and bring heaven to earth.

Most people have still not yet observed or admitted that their daily struggles to attain more money or higher positions or finer possessions or deeper relationships give them only brief glimpses of peace. Even after accomplishing some long sought physical or mental or social goal, the taste of peace that such outer accomplishments give quickly dissipates. Only with constant effort and revisiting of past victories do such accomplishments give further tastes of peace. (And such small "remembered" tastes are not in themselves fulfilling, or nourishing!)

And of course, I have nothing against making more money, or attaining promotions or having fine possessions. Such are the natural fruits of our labors! And great accomplishments—physical, mental and social—are the delightful spices of life! Still, we must all at some point glimpse the life-changing truth that the practice of the presence of peace is the *means* to such attainments, such accomplishments, and not the *result* of such accomplishments. Without an awareness from

130

the *beginning* of the presence of peace, and a continuing awareness of our peace throughout the process, then such attainments and accomplishments will prove to be shallow, unsatisfactory and empty. The person who succeeds in making the practice of peace his/her *primary* goal, and motivating energy, will discover that financial, social and physical rewards naturally blossom, not as the target but as the bi-product of life's peaceable activity.

Recognizing the presence of peace as a constant companion, we discover that our work is most often accomplished expertly and on time (indeed, often *ahead* of schedule!). When we make the awareness of peace our highest priority, all of our other obligations find their proper place and season. The prize is never far off, but is won moment by moment. To subordinate all other ambitions to the quest for the "peace prize" requires the courage of a spiritual warrior. Again, the scriptures suggest the true disciple must leave house and family to follow the Lord — the Law of Peace. We do not need to physically leave our house and family. Rather, we leave behind our faith in house and family as a means to peace, and instead follow the inner law — the inner Lord — of love, of peace. This is a moment by moment departure from worldly turmoils, and a moment by moment holding to the peace which is prior to everything that arises.

To be in constant communion, or constant conversation with peace, is to live the most exalted, most beautiful yet most simple and tender life possible. And the most serviceable. The truth of these words can only be proven by those who would embark on the voyage of such constant communion with, such unceasing attention to, the presence of peace.

My experience is that peace is our native state of being. To commune with this peace, converse with this peace is the final stage before duality is dissolved and the presence of peace itself is all that lives. To perceive peace as a presence in which we might rest, or a companion with whom we might converse, is surely not to demean or diminish the nature of peace. Rather, such resting, and such dialogues are a few of the methods we can use to make peace more tangible, more accessible to our daily awareness.

My own long experience assures me I am justified, and emboldened when I converse with peace, or rest in peace in this way.

If I were a teacher, or an employer, or a coach, I would instruct those under my charge to begin this habitual conversation with peace, to begin this practice of remembering the presence of peace. If I were a legislator, or a governor, I would pass laws directing the populace to this work, for it is the most useful, most natural and most efficient, and yet the most underutilized practice on earth.

The eternal presence of peace waits for each of us "closer than our breath," with all the treasures of heaven, if we would but turn our gaze in Her direction. And as we do so, as we learn and train ourselves to attend to her soft inner light, we are quickly confirmed in our efforts, and from this point a lifelong devotion, an ever-increasing commitment spontaneously springs forth. To attend to the presence of peace is to attend to the fires of life. To forget this presence, or to make it a lesser priority, is to let the flames dwindle and depart. We can abandon everything for the sake of attending to peace, which we do simply by being at peace with the thoughts we are thinking, which inevitably leads to peaceable feelings. We are free to drop or ignore all thoughts and feelings with which we are not at peace. (We get better and better at this as we practice.) This is the simple inner discipline we are called to, which brings heaven to earth, and lifts the earthbound to heaven.

This simple practice—of holding in consciousness only those thoughts with which we are at peace, whether these thoughts are engaged for a brief moment, or an uninterrupted hour—proves itself beneficial both in our immediate experience and over the long journey of a lifetime. We feel the results of this practice not only in our thoughts and feelings but also in our bodies, and in our every relationship, and in our work activities and our leisurely pursuits.

Clear enough? Simple enough? I trust you will, and already have shared similar insights and encouragements with our dear lady, Grace. Which leads me to confess, of course, that I still enjoy all of my thoughts about her, and you, good friend. Let this joy be my prayer for you, and her. As you enjoy your thoughts of me, are at peace with your thoughts, you likewise are praying. We pray this way for each other, and all others, with our peace. It is peace that has brought us together in thought and spirit as well as in physical companionship. Our lives are touched by this light, and never again need the shadows overwhelm us.

Practicing the Presence of Peace

Please share these sentiments, as you are so prompted, with our dear lady friend.

I remain with you, in peace and in joy —

(*Charlie*)

Sixth Letter:
This Is the Most Practical Daily Activity

Hello, (Shawna J.) (Residing in a drug rehabilitation facility)

Thank you for the gifts and for your encouragements. We are indeed true companions in the presence of peace. I am inspired by seeing someone so young who is so mature in the discipline of accessing this peaceable presence. I am tickled to hear you confess that your direct inner experience of peace leaves you somewhat bored with your old habits—the "false promises of sense stimulations," as you so adroitly put it.

We can of course admit that our physical senses are a wonder and a grace, revealing many of the treasures of life to us. But we can also observe that they do so only because we are first connected with an inner presence— a transcendent Presence—that does not rely on such sense impressions. I intuit from your letters that that you are deepening your acquaintance with this inner Presence.

As you might guess, I see many people every day who do not attend to the peaceable presence. To me this is as if they had neglected to bathe, or brush their teeth or change their clothes. To choose thoughts with which you are at peace and to release thoughts with which you are not at peace is to me the most basic, most practical, and the most necessary of all daily activities. We are invited to retire from all other concerns to spend our time with the presence of peace. In such retirement we need only act or speak or think when peaceable presence prompts us to act, or speak or think. When we are in communion with peace, or in conversation with peace, we then move through our day world without fear or hesitancy, clear in our mind and gentle in our touch and strong in our work. When we forget the peaceable presence, or are distracted by the suggestion of some complicated unhappiness, we become sluggish, and cloudy in mind and clumsy in touch and inefficient in our work. We can learn to return to peace, to rely on peace, to remain with peace—all the day—for our own good and for the good of all others around us.

You will discover that such an exercise rejuvenates your body. Your past mistreatments, or "trashing," of your body, as you put it, does not limit the healing ministrations or empowerment of the presence of peace. With peace as your already present companion, you are no longer driven to constantly stimulate the body with food or intoxicants or personal or social pleasures or dramas. Although with peace nothing is forbidden, one quickly discovers that with an awareness if the immediacy of peace nothing else is needed. I find that I do not consciously deprive myself

136

of these "secondary pleasures," e.g. drugs, sex and rock and roll, on one end of the spectrum, and prayer, meditation and exercise on the other end. Although I do not deprive myself of these "sense stimulators," neither do I seek them out. I find myself simply happy to breathe, to see, to smell, to hear, enjoying the moments of my daily life either alone or with others. Peace is not a jealous companion, and thus She is also a sufficient companion.

As you suggest, on occasion, you might find it enjoyable to take up various secondary disciplines— with your diet or with physical exercises or sexual abstinence or sexual explorations or formal sessions, short or long of prayer and mediation. When you are in peace, you are free to explore all manner of behavior, with intensity or flippancy, or moderation or exaggeration according to your taste. As you remain conscious of your primary focus—practicing the presence of peace, by simply being at peace with the thoughts you are thinking—then your behavior is spontaneously balanced, appropriate, healthy.

As we've discussed, we bring ourselves back to the presence of peace time and time again throughout the day by simply asking, "Am I at peace with these thoughts, yes or no?" If the answer is not an immediate and spontaneous *yes*, it's a *no*.

When we are at peace with our thoughts, we are at peace. If we are not at peace with our thoughts, then we either *choose* to be at peace with them or choose to drop those thoughts and find or create thoughts with which we are more at peace. (Simple to describe—a lifetime to master!)

As you return to this process again and again, you'll find yourself living by Grace, moved by Spirit, serving others and the world at large with spontaneous love, lightness, and devotion. This would seem to be the goal you said you were aiming toward in your letter to me.

A quick observation: you do not have to have *faith* in the presence of peace, or even an understanding that your own experience of peace is the individual experience of God's Universal Spirit (which is how I now understand it.) What you most need is the direct *experience* of peace, (even a small grain of it!) and more pointedly, the direct experience of how you, yourself, might consciously open to the presence of peace, moment by moment, thought by thought. The other side of this same coin is the direct experience of consciously *releasing unhappiness*, releasing turmoil, again, moment by moment, and thought by thought. Such direct experience arising again and again in your daily life will naturally, inevitably lead to faith and understanding, and an ever-deepening practice.

Your momentary experience of peace, and more especially the experience of being able to *choose* peace moment by moment, regardless of the situation, releases you from the necessity of engaging in many activities which in the past were engaged as *means* to the end, e.g., as a means to a sense of peace. Pursuits of food, sex, money, social standing, political power — or even beauty itself — all of which have been pursued for millennia as means to the end of happiness, or peace — such pursuits lose their aberrant immediacy, their blind driving force, when the end — a sense of peace — is

138

already present, already one's moment by moment experience. This does not mean that you do not continue to enjoy food, sex, money, social standing, political power and beauty itself. On the contrary, knowing peace first, these secondary experiences often are *more* available and absolutely more enjoyable than when peace is a hit or miss target. Consciously enjoying the innate, natural presence of peace which is within you is what brings balance and dignity into your outer life. Peace is the *means*, and not the end of a well-lived life.

We must be clear, again, however, that we recognize that the presence of peace is not a "usable" presence — to be "used" for the attainment of money, food, sex, etc. The presence of peace is always sufficient unto itself, self-supporting, complete, at ease. The urge to "use" peace in order to gain some other supposed good end is only the momentum of previous disciplines being carried over to the new discipline of peace. Curiously enough, you can not "use" peace for anything whatsoever — you can only enjoy it. When you try to *use* peace, you lose it. When you *follow* peace, then peace *uses you* to express Its perfect Presence.

As practitioners of peace, we continue in the world, enjoying all of the wonders and simple delights as well as the opportunities and wide-ranging potentials. We engage in business and sports and family life and politics and whatever our interest leads us to. But we continue because we *are* complete, and not in search of completion.

Practicing the presence of peace is a gentle, easy, non-violent approach to ourselves and the world which

139

contrasts sharply with the stern, aggressive approach which has been dominant in our culture (and around the world) for many millennia. Such an aggressive approach was perhaps necessary and appropriate for those previous generations—or at least allowable, from a soul's eternal perspective. I am absolutely confident that further human progress on earth will now be made most rapidly through the vision of the presence of peace and the immediate practicality of this peace in our daily lives. (I sense we share this vision!)

By monitoring your thoughts, one by one, moment by moment, you learn again to be kind to yourself, to be gentle and forgiving, and patient and tender. Until now we have each carried and used the sharp sticks and knives and clubs of our ancestors, carrying and using those thoughts which puncture and pierce and brutalize our view of ourselves and the world. Such warfare is no longer necessary. Practicing the presence of peace is enjoying an armistice, an armistice that brings peace not only into our own lives but also into the world at large. Where else could peace possibly originate?

The practice of being at peace with your thoughts gives you, to one degree or another, immediate release from pain and sorrow, and provides you with the immediate rewards of abundant supply, friendly support and clear understanding. It is in this way that the means and the ends of your life are harmonized. The practice of peace is a practice which you can faithfully engage through your whole life, up to the moment of death itself and into life eternal, where the practice will continue to guide you into ever higher spheres. Peace is that eternal presence within you that brings you face to face with the Father-Mother Creator-Sustainer. You see this One, first, "though a glass darkly," and then as you learn to more fully accept this peaceable presence, as you train to receive ever deeper draughts, you perceive Your Beloved quite clearly, in full daylight, with no veils, or illusions or shadows of doubt. Peace stands with you in this first moment of your practice—indeed, even before you practice—and remains with you as you mature into eternity.

We are companions in this work, Shawna, so we can be at peace with each other and enjoy each other in these processes, and in these practices. The community which we spontaneously bring together through our attention to peace is the true brotherhood and sisterhood which has been potentialed from the beginning of time. I am delighted to be sharing it with you. Please hold me in your thoughts with tenderness.

In Joy and Light.... Your friend...

(Charlie)

Seventh Letter:
As You Are Healed, the World Is Healed

Hello, Linda (In the hospital) —

Of course, dear friend, I am more than happy to offer you here a few "instructions," as you put it, and whatever words of advice and encouragement to help you get back on your feet. I trust the process will be quick, and that you'll be back soon.

When someone appears to be having great difficulties, such as you now face, it is usual for their friends to offer support by saying, "I love you, I stand with you, I'm praying for you." And in fact, I do love you, Linda, and stand by you and pray for you. We are in this together. However, I sense that what I mean by these particular words is much clearer in my own mind and more immediate than is common when most people use them.

I have come to recognize that "love" and "the presence of peace" are all words pointing to the exact same thing. I am at peace with you, lady, not because of the troubles you are facing, but for the simple, delicious

142

fact of your being. I am at peace with the beauty of your individuality, the friendliness of your spirit, the deep mystery of your adventure here. In this regard, and may it not sound callous, I am at peace with your bravery, your boldness in taking on a portion of the sufferings of the world, and working them out through your life, dissolving them with your current work. (As you are healed, the world is healed.) I know that peace itself is your true nature, and I feel honored by your continuing presence in the midst of that which would deny such nature.

I stand with you by standing with—perceiving—your peace. What you may be experiencing as physical troubles and pain and suffering, I know to be only the temporary surface appearance of your true condition, which is abiding in peace, harmony and beauty. And this is how I pray for you—by recognizing the presence of peace as omnipotent and omnipresent, and right where you are, all the time, all the day. I hold my thoughts to the truth of this presence regardless of the physical appearances, and this holding of thought in the presence of peace is how I pray to support you.

I encourage you to arrange all of your daily affairs, both in and out of the hospital, in accordance with the peace you experience in them. Let peace guide you to what next to do, what to leave behind. This is actually very easy, very natural and ordinary, and is the quickest path to the restoration of harmony in your experience.

Remembering the presence of peace is the most practical thing you can do for yourself and for all others. Remembering peace is the same thing as remembering "health and well-being." Seeing, feeling, experiencing the presence of peace not only within your own consciousness but also in all that you encounter is the grace by which all suffering is resolved. When you train yourself to constantly watch for it, you discover that peace is a palpable presence, indeed, it is awareness itself. To simply allow the presence of peace to be what it already is takes no great effort or intellectual leap. Peace is present for its own sake — self sustaining, self-sufficient, self-evolving.

You may want to play "companion" with the presence of peace, act as though this presence were your best friend, or twin, with whom you could share all of your life's moments, the ups and downs, lights and darks, certainties and uncertainties. The peaceable presence *will* respond to your play, your game, and guide you, tabernacle with you, to whatever extent you allow.

The experience of peace which comes as you make peace with the thoughts you are thinking is the single most effective curative agent. It is a medicine that can be taken hundreds of times a day with increasingly benign, beneficent effects. Take a dose upon waking, and another as you sit up, and yet another as your feet hit the floor. Take a dose with the start of every meal and with the middle of the meal and at the end of the meal. Take extra doses before bed.

You see my point here: Peace is willing to nurse you around the clock, guide and support you in all that you do. Let Her do it!

If you claim ignorance as to exactly how to let peace minister to you in this way, be at peace with your ignorance! Then ask peace to inform you, ask her to teach you, step by step. This is the most important study on earth. If you are a slow learner, be at peace with being a slow learner! If you forget to bring peace in at every breath, be at peace with your forgetfulness.

If you take a one inch step towards peace, she leaps five feet in your direction! If you whisper a single word of your willingness to learn from her, she'll sing her instructions for hours. She is here with you, always, and is Herself made more beautiful and more empowered by your simple remembrances.

Peace is not so much a philosophy or a belief system or a spiritual insight as it is a living, unceasing though invisible Presence. We may go to church to contact this Presence, though we may also simply wait a moment during our day-life—be it at a red light or in line at the supermarket or during the rush of ordinary work activities. We simply wait a moment and consciously reconnect with this Invisible Presence which is peace. This peace is our very essence. Such pausing to wait on peace is a natural rhythm, an ordinary "refueling" as necessary as breathing and eating.

I have no doubt that every human being has the presence of peace at his or her center, and thus everybody has the need and the capacity for turning to peace for life's sustenance. Peace is an intelligent presence at the center of our being, and is thus intimately familiar with each of our histories, and our present complexities and fears and desires for the future. Each time we turn to this center, this peaceable presence — be such turning spontaneous in the moment or extensively planned and formal — each turning elicits the precisely right form, or expression from peace which will take us the next step, or leap or provide us with the perfect confirmation in our journey. We are perfectly instructed and aligned in peace, by Peace Herself. She brings us all the courage and insight and energy and intelligence necessary — and *more* than is necessary — to experience life fully, radiating beauty and power, integrity and love.

The peaceable presence acts as our insurance agent, meeting all our claims in order to extend our years, enhance our usefulness, protect and confirm our wealth. In peace, our lives simplify and yet our services to others multiply, and thus we increasingly experience an abundance of all that is good. Without peace, we have no richness, no friendship, no love, no real power or direction. Practicing the presence of peace is the secret to a rich and healthy life. Have I made this clear? Can we share this understanding?

Make your journey into peace conscious, deliberate, decisive. It's actually quite simple. You *choose* to give credence only to those thoughts with which you are at peace and you *choose* to abandon thoughts with which you are not at peace, thoughts which cause division and opposition. You *choose* to not tell yourself or anyone else stories about other people, places, circumstances or events with which you are not at peace. You *choose* to now be at peace with many of the thoughts that perhaps in the past, or according to custom have caused upset or frustration.

You do this moment by moment, in your business environment and in your family affairs and in your personal times. Relying on peace itself, you are not bound by tradition but only by the integrity and freedom which this presence includes. You are free to be at peace with the conventions of our age, and just as free to be at peace with radically new forms of thinking, feeling, and acting. Let peace itself be your tender guide, your compassionate instructor, your careful guardian. No one is ever hurt by such guidance and loving ministrations. Through ordinary daily experience you soon learn to trust your peace, and to move quickly and boldly under its prompting. And the world is brightened, and more peaceable, more lovely because of your discipline.

Dear Linda, when I think of you, my joy is steady. Please remember me this way, with joy, and peace. We serve each other this way. I'll see you again, soon, and again we'll take up our eternal dialogue!

Our peace is one presence...

(*Charlie*)

Eighth Letter:
Go Easy on Yourself

Hello, Dear Molly —

(In reply to her letter concerning difficulty in releasing thoughts with which she was not at peace.)

Go easy on yourself, good friend! Most people in the world have long been accustomed to holding thoughts with which they are not comfortable, thoughts that cause division and frustration and fear. Indeed, we even teach our children this very (black) art. And we do so because our grandfathers and great grandfathers and great-great-great grandfathers, on back through history, were trained and accustomed to hold thoughts which they did not enjoy and which caused them grief. Thus, your complaint about these "unwelcome visitors" is neither unusual nor unexpected. The difficulty you face with such visitors is the difficulty most people in the world encounter in our time.

If we are going to take up the peace practice, we have, as you know, two choices when such thoughts appear:

148

1.) we can choose to release such thoughts and replace them with thoughts with which we are more comfortable, more at peace; or 2.) we can choose to *be at peace* with the thoughts that a moment before caused the upset. It really makes no difference which choice we make. Both choices are premised on the understanding that being at peace with our thoughts—immediately, spontaneously—is the most practical and empowering thing we can do for ourselves and for all those around us.

These two choices—this ongoing practice—replaces the world's (normal) tradition and training of "chewing" on the thoughts we do not enjoy, that cause us worry and anxiety. Most people hold to such thoughts—extending, rearranging and detailing them, trying to make them come out different. This normal practice of chewing on thoughts that cause us trouble is based on the assumption that at some point, in the near or distant future, we will be forced to change, confront or rearrange the outer *objects* of our troubled thinking—whether we are thinking about our spouse, our children, our job, our government, or "them over there." We chew over these things because we assume that at some point we will need to change something "out there" in order to finally be at peace in our lives. This is a faulty assumption.

It's faulty because peace is much closer at hand, and requires nothing to change in the outer world before showing its face. We reconnect with peace simply by engaging either one of the two inner choices mentioned above. It has nothing to do with changing the outer world.

As you might suspect, one of the arguments I regularly encounter against this method is that if we continually put our attention on just monitoring our own thoughts, we will be abandoning our "duty" to outer responsibilities, and neglect efforts to bring peace and justice to the outer world. In other words, we have been taught that it is our *duty* to hold to thoughts which we do not enjoy, and struggle to change the *objects* of our thoughts in order to bring justice and compassion into the world. This argument is one of the factors which sometimes inhibits beginning practitioners from radically embracing the methods here offered.

I generally refrain from arguing my case and instead encourage people just to try it and experience for themselves the outer results. As we hold to the presence of peace, we soon discover that peace and justice are the natural result of our practice. Indeed, we find ourselves moving much more quickly, efficiently, and boldly in the causes of peace and justice than ever we moved while thinking thoughts that caused us grief. As a general rule, the universe *empowers* those who are at peace with their thoughts and subdues those who are not at peace with their thoughts. Thus in the scripture, "To those who have, it will be given, and to those who do not have, it will be taken away."

The point of this, my friend, is that you *do* have a choice as to what you will think, as to the thoughts you entertain. You are empowered to choose to be at peace with a thought which a moment before you were not at peace. You are empowered to release a thought which troubles you. However, you have to *exercise* this power.

And the more you exercise it, the more of it you have. (It does take practice!)

In the beginning of your practice it may seem as though you are constantly being presented with thoughts you do not enjoy, that trouble you or cause frustration. At first it seems that this practice requires you to interrupt *all* your traditional (acquired) thinking habits. And in fact this may be the case. If you have only seldom or accidentally discovered and held to thoughts that you enjoy, with which you are at peace, then the practice of doing so consistently must be built up step by step (thought by thought). As your practice matures, however, you will discover that being at peace with your thoughts—and consciously choosing thoughts with which you can be at peace—is the most natural, liberating and easy practice you would ever engage. You will soon find yourself moving through whole days, and then entire weeks with increasing peace, without experiencing any unhappiness whatsoever. But that is not the object. The object is simply to be at peace in *this* moment, by being at peace with this thought, right now, right here. The days and weeks will take care of themselves.

I have suggested two methods for being at peace with your thoughts: 1.) choosing to be at peace with a thought which a moment before caused you trouble or anxiety (i.e., thoughts such as, *You're fired!* or *I'm good for nothing*, or *It's snowing again!*); and 2.) simply choosing a thought which is more comfortable than the first thought.

As I said, neither of these methods is inherently better or more efficient than the other, since the experience of peace is the only test for our efficiency. The first option, however, is a much less common practice and often provides new and unexpected territories to explore. To be at peace with such thoughts as, *I've just been fired!* or *I'm good for nothing!* or *It's snowing again* is not an ordinary attitude to take, and yet it is the most empowering, the most healthful attitude of all.

You are not obliged to be at peace with *every* thought which comes up. Some thoughts are simply too far away from our customary "peace zone" to be included. In such situations, the second option is immediately available. The more you practice, however, the larger your "peace zone" becomes, and the more service you are able to offer the world. ("The presence of peace" is a basic life-service which we have to offer each other and the environment. "Love" and "peace" are two words for the same Presence!)

I do not mean to make this process — these methods — appear complicated or difficult. In fact, they are quite simple, ordinary, requiring few words, little effort. Peace is already present in consciousness, and you simply acknowledge it in your thinking, one way or another. When you have forgotten peace — when you are not at peace with your thoughts — you can simply stop, wait, like a person whose dog is running loose, or playing "catch me." In fact, it is easier to catch your peace than to catch the dog! As you stop, wait, remind yourself that being at peace really is the most practical thing for you and for everybody else, and that you are at peace when you are peace with the thoughts you're thinking, your awareness naturally returns to peace.

You can think of the peace presence as your employer, by whom you are employed twenty-four hours a day, seven days a week. You will soon discover there is no other work, no other occupation as rewarding, as rejuvenating, as endlessly varying, as easy or interesting as attending to peace moment by moment, thought after thought. And yet, if and when you take time off from this employment, such absence need not itself be cause for worry and strife. You simply return to the job—and find your employer has not missed you, and holds you in no disgrace or disadvantage. Peace remains peace, unaffected by your absence, and thus encouraging you even more to remain faithfully on the task. You soon learn there is no other place you want to be, no other work you want to do. Peace builds up in your life until you are drowned, submerged, completely saturated with Her effulgence.

Practicing peace—even by the simple, somewhat mechanical method of remembering, or reciting the principles and the practice—becomes an habitual practice because of the natural drawing power of Peace Herself. Here is a simple and powerful observation yet one that is seldom made: experiencing peace is easier and more expansive than experiencing doubts, confusion, despair, pain and suffering. And contrary to the world's teaching, our practice confirms that the experience of peace or the experience of suffering is (99% of the time) in fact a *choice*, and the choice of experience is solely made in the thoughts one chooses to entertain, moment by moment, day after day. It is not a choice between "right thoughts" or "wrong thoughts," or "true thoughts" or "untrue thoughts." And it is most especially not a choice between "peaceful thoughts" and "un-peaceful thoughts." We recognize that thoughts themselves are neither peaceful nor un-peaceful, true or untrue, right or wrong. Rather, it is a matter of whether you, personally, individually, are *at peace* with a particular thought or not. Simply recognize that there are thoughts you, personally, enjoy to think and thoughts you, personally, do not (at this moment) enjoy to think. Regardless of your choice of thoughts, you learn more and more to remain always with your own personal sense of peace, of joy, and whatever thought you are most at peace with at this moment or about this subject is the thought you are free to think. This practice is in fact quite easy, natural and enlightening. When given half a chance this practice quickly becomes a way of life. It's a no-brainer: do you choose to suffer, or be at peace? And after some practice, surprise of surprises, Peace quietly reveals Herself as our fundamental state of being. The practice takes us home!

To live your days "at home," in natural awareness of your fundamental state of being—which is peace itself—brings uncountable blessings and advantages, not only for yourself but for all those around you, and to the very earth upon which you walk.

I must bring this to a close. We support each other, dear Molly, in this peaceable work, by enjoying our thoughts of each other, being at peace with our thoughts, and remaining steadfast in our practice whether apart or together.

So in peace, we are always together —

(Charlie)

Ninth Letter:
Be at Peace with the Beginner's Circumstance

$\mathbb{H}$i Bill —

Jenny Larsen, one of your clients, wrote to say she was quite taken by my talk the other day and has asked me to help her with what she describes as her "beginner's circumstance." I replied and told her I would be happy to help, but that I would do so through you, as her therapist. I told her you, too, had been practicing this way for some time, and that is why you asked me to share my experience with your group. So here is my response to Jenny's "beginner's circumstance," which I trust you will convey to her (and others who might be interested.)

In her letter Jenny said she wanted to move quickly along the "Path of Peace," as my talk had been titled, but that she was very much a beginner in these things, and was uncertain how to proceed. So my basic suggestion is that she *be at peace* with her beginner's circumstance, *be at peace* with her uncertainty, *be at peace* with her apprenticeship, *be at peace* with the process itself, *be at peace* with her first groping to glimpse her true nature. We don't wait for peace on this path. We *start* with it, if only a mustard seed's worth. .

In fact, though, we already have it all. My understanding is that she, and all of us, are always completely submerged, engulfed in an infinite blaze of peace. The light within each of our billions of atoms is peace itself. Thus, none of us are ever obliged to *become* peaceful, any more than sunlight is obliged to *become* warm! We share our nature with each other, and support and encourage each other to rely on, rest in this original energy (peace!). Sometimes we employ specific words of instruction and guidance, as I do right here. More often, what we share is simply our easy, ordinary presence—our ordinary self, our ordinary being—which we offer spontaneously, effortlessly, as naturally as water offers itself downhill. Since peace is our nature, we can trust it to in-form itself into whatever form—shape—is necessary for the moment's demand. (So I trust you will keep me *in-form-ed* of Jenny's progress, of her condition, as you are so moved by your own peace, and, of course, only to the degree that professional courtesy and ethics might prompt.)

Professional practice aside, more and more I recognize that the only responsibility any of us have here on earth is to be at peace with our thoughts, moment by moment, minute by minute, hour after hour. My experience is that when we fulfill this basic responsibility—to be at peace with our thoughts—we are spontaneously led to what has traditionally been viewed as right action, right relationship, right discipline, within and without. My understanding now is that practicing peace, enjoying the peace, was the purpose of our birth, the purpose of our maturity, the purpose of our work, our play and our intimate relations and social engagements. We have no responsibility outside of peace. The presence of peace is a simple fact of our existence, yet this simple fact implies a lifetime of demonstration with the resultant crumbling, from such demonstration, of thousands of years of warring, unhappy traditions.

Contrary to our social conditioning, I now understand that whenever I refuse to assume responsibility for those things (people, relationships, activities) in which I have no peace, I am quietly agreeing to further the suffering of humanity. Enough of that! Responsibility without peace is a dark momentum left over from past warring and unhappy generations. We have all carried such momentum, such warring darkness, in our bodies, as well as in our mental and emotional atmospheres and intimate social relations. I am quite certain that we need not carry these burdens from the past—this faulty conditioning—any further. When we recognize such unwelcome passengers—anxieties, frustrations, unhappiness—in the course of fulfilling some responsibility we have assumed, we are now empowered to refuse any further transit to these passengers. And as we do so, the generations ahead are lightened of their load.

We abandon unhappy responsibilities an inch at a time, moment by moment, by releasing those thoughts with which we are not at peace, which continue the warfare and turmoil. Through this process, long-held and unwelcome responsibilities naturally dissolve, or suddenly disappear, but always gracefully, harmoniously, blessing one and all alike. My releasing of un-peaceable responsibilities never burdens someone else for my release is done for all of us, for all of humanity. Inch by inch, thought by thought, I release those thoughts with which I am not at peace or I simply choose to be at peace with what a moment before (or a generation before) I could not enjoy. Peace is the key. Peace is the only responsibility.

We are all beginners in this work, in this generation. I am happy to think that the peace which our children and grandchildren and great grandchildren will know far exceeds what we might now imagine. And they, in their turn will be beginners in comparison to those who come after them. Peace has no limits to Her potential expressions.

And yet, as we assume our responsibility for peace — thought by thought, inch by inch — we are mature, just as pioneers were mature in their courage and hope and ambition. Sufficient unto the day is the peace here given. Our fragile bodies would explode, our delicate minds shatter were we forced to experience the magnitude of the peaceable presence in store for future generations. Inch by inch, thought by thought, our peace is sufficient, our responsibilities are fulfilled. Each moment is a sufficient and appropriate place to begin our work anew. At any moment we might ask, "What am I thinking right now? What would I *enjoy* to think right now?" And the work of the millennium is again taken up. If our thoughts are of the past, then our peace is repairing the past. If we are thinking of the moment's circumstance, then our peace opens the door right now for heaven on earth. If our thoughts are of the future, we build a paradise through the peaceable presence for ourselves and for the new generations. Peace is appropriate regardless of the content or time-frame of our thoughts. Peace does not register how long we have been away from Her. She gives Herself completely, no matter how long we have forgotten Her, and no matter how much of Her we are not yet able to accept.

Our work—our responsibility—is not only in the continual recognition and acceptance of the peaceable presence as the fundamental nature of life and this as our own fundamental nature. Our work is simultaneously the quick recognition and denial of all that is unlike peace. The long rule of the warring imposter deserves no more of our allegiance, not one further moment's service.

We are designed to be at peace with all of our thoughts without interruption. We are free to train ourselves to do exactly this. We learn to trust in and rely on the presence of peace for every detail of our lives. The reward of such trust is not long in coming. The immediate experience of peace is its own and sufficient reward, and yet peace continues to pour out Her gifts and kindnesses and delights in form after form, expected and unexpected. Through the moment by moment experience of the presence of peace, the kingdom of heaven is awakened here on earth and all things become possible to us. Denying our peace, we deny life itself.

Peace is not only the grease which keeps life's wheels turning, it is also the Cosmic Engine which originally created and moved the wheels! And yet, peace is not just a mechanical force, but a sentient, intelligent, self-aware Presence. To ignore Her is to ignore the safety precautions, the training manual, and the Rules of Procedure for our individual lives. We are free to ignore these basic mechanics of life, but why would we?

Our own momentary, individualized experience of the presence of peace is our gateway to the eternal, impersonal peace here extant. As we listen for and respond to our own inner sense of peace, we simultaneously attend to the eternal order. Our work, our responsibility on earth is in such attendance. We take up our work, take up our responsibility at every moment by being at peace with the thoughts we are thinking—and dismissing or recontextualizing those with which we are not at peace. This is not something we do only in prayer, or when we're in trouble, but always, every day, all day.

You may complain that my teaching is too simple, and I'm overly repetitive. You're right, of course. Nevertheless, my experience is that this teaching—being at peace with your thoughts—is absolutely sufficient, and since I continually practice it myself, with such sweet and heart-melting rewards, delights, I again and again encourage all who will listen—begin! begin! Test for yourself this most ancient and here renewed inner custom. Verify my words in your own experience. See if my exuberance is not well-founded!

The presence of peace is the presence of love. Love is peace. Two words for the same presence, the same divine condition. I call the world to love. Be at peace with the thoughts you are thinking, the feelings you are feeling. Why waste precious time with thoughts that bring you suffering? With feelings that you are not happy to feel? You *are* gracefully, inherently *empowered* to engage this moment by moment exercise.

Let us return, quickly, subtly, peaceably, time and again to the presence that resides in our hearts and minds. Why should I need to plead for you to sample such heavenly indulgences? Our earth has long been covered in darkness and suffering. When we come out of darkness, the light at first strains our eyes, retouches old wounds. Yet the relief is welcome!

You will discover that this method has the effect much like a parent reassuring a child in the night: "it's alright, it's alright, wake up, drink, quench your thirst. What is real is here, now, in front of you. And it is love. It is peace. You are safe. Unharmed. The world is at rest."

This waking to what is real is the experience of those who take up this work, who assume their peaceable responsibilities — their responsibility for remembering the peace within.

Thank you again, friend, for inviting me to your group and allowing me once again to consider these matters with you and yours in this way. I trust we'll continue in this work together for eons!

I am yours, in Peace, Joy and Good Company —

(*Charlie*)

162

Tenth Letter:
Staying Connected Eases the Other's Distress

Hello again, Mrs. Thornton—

I trust you are well. Thank you for your encouragement and advice. Alas, contrary to your hopes, the grief which John is now exhibiting after losing his long-time friend and companion does not, I confess, motivate me to seek him out to share the work that I have been sharing with you and others. In fact, I intuit that his animated display of grief, at what he experiences as an overwhelming loss and his consistent appeal for sympathy, is in truth his form of "peace" in this season—something he needs to do to find his own balance. I am not moved to disengage him from it. You yourself, of course, are free to share with him whatever of our work you feel is appropriate, be it in my words or yours, following your own sense of the presence of peace.

Your urge to help him is honorable. I suspect that you are experiencing more and more the life-enhancing, death-defying peace which this work gives to those who engage it, and it is for this reason that you want John to have a share of it. I am confident that you will continue to discover the appropriateness of peace, either spoken or unspoken, in every circumstance, including and especially those circumstances which seem most dark and sorrowful. To keep hold of one's peace in such circumstances is not a lack of sympathy or compassion but in fact the highest sympathy, relying on the highest truth, and the deepest compassion. Staying connected with that which is deepest, most true within us does not magnify but rather eases the distress of others. To be at peace with what you are thinking lights the path which leads through the "valley of the shadow of death." You are more and more faithful to this light, and because of your faith your spontaneous service to others, such as to John, in his current season of grief, will be easy and sure.

Practicing the presence of peace continues to bring us ever deeper and more fulfilling relationships. To recognize that this presence is the source of all good that has come to us from without, is to align ourselves with unending grace. The love and friendship that John experienced with his companion was an outer expression of the inner peace which resided within each of them individually. To truly honor that friendship necessitates the recognition of the *source* of that friendship. To grieve, and feel a human sense of loss when our friend, companion and lover has gone is quite natural and without blame. Yet deep maturity in our intimate relationships leads us to experience a joy, strength and wisdom that inspires us to remain committed to peace, committed to friendship, regardless of the claims of our physical senses. It is only the physical senses which falsely deny this friendship's continuity. When we fully recognize that peace (Peace) is the source of our friendship, companionship and intimacy, we can then also recognize that nothing is truly lost when death tries to interrupt. Peace is awareness itself, and though the forms that arise in this peaceable awareness continue to change, its peaceable essence abides eternally. Grief and feelings of loss have their rightful seasons, yet our peace is not thereby diminished.

As a gift to John let us assume — choose to think — that fulfilling friendships will continue to arise for him, even though they will, of course, be different than the friendship he has had with his friend. We are free to be at peace with our thoughts about John, so I choose to think that this season of grief is simply preparing him for a season of fulfillment. Such fulfillment is the nature of life, the nature of the presence of peace. As John remains with this presence (no matter what form that presence takes!) new friendships will arise on the foundation which was built by this friendship which is now — not past, but rather invisible.

I am convinced, by my own experience, that the decision to both enter and exit this realm is made, or at least agreed to, at the fundamental level of the soul. In some way we choose the right time to both enter and exit this earthly realm. With such an understanding I would suggest that at some level John's friend willingly participated in his own exit from this world. John is free to honor his friend's decision — his friend's earthly destiny — with peace and insight.

We need not burden our friends (or lovers or companions or family members) with the obligation of bringing us peace. We of course can and do enjoy our friends, our lovers and family members. Yet we unburden them and ourselves when recognize that they only *elicit* our joy, our peace. By their presence they each express and reflect unique qualities of that which is already within us, e.g., the peaceable presence, which is awareness itself. Others are not truly the *source* of our joy, our peace. When we begin to view anyone or anything as the *source* of our peace, we diminish our peace, and this creates an imbalance which sooner or later must be rectified. The peaceable presence which is at the heart of each of us, which constitutes each of our natural, ordinary selves, is what attracts our friends and lovers, and it is what we have to offer them. Let us hold up our end of the relationship by always returning to, remaining with the natural and un-possessive peace which we are. In such balance, friendships flourish through eternity.

Devotion to the presence of peace is not a complicated, long and drawn out process but rather a simple moment by moment, thought by thought practice. Anything which would irritate, annoy, upset or anger us in this moment is a direct result of a *thought* with which are not at peace. Yes, these thoughts may be generated by outside circumstances or relationships, yet the thoughts themselves are rising up within. Always and immediately our peace is available to us, and it is the discipline of accessing the inner presence of peace that, with practice, brings peace to the entire world.

Let's imagine that for many years you had longed for the return of a particular lover. You secretly hoped that somehow, some way each of your life's circumstances would change such that you were brought together again at just the right time and place, with no other relationship commitments, so that you might begin again a tender relationship that had for some reason ended. Now let's imagine that this is exactly what happens. Will you have the courage to actually fulfill your secret longing, to move in the direction of your heart's desire, here in the real world, in real time?

Let me suggest that such is the case right now with the presence of peace. Your long lost lover is here! The time is right. The place is right. Your lover is willing. Your lover reaches out a tentative hand. Reach for it! Hold it! Do not let it go! There is no other time but now! Your life is about to begin again.

This lover is now rich, and powerful, and wise. As human beings here on this earth it is our moment by moment devotion to the presence of peace that inevitably results in the ongoing supply of all else we need—home, food, friends, good work, harmonious family life, social involvement, responsibility and respect. To seek any of these by abandoning our relationship with peace is destructive foolishness, though such abandonment has been our general custom for generations.

Our role in life, and our secret devotion, our true passion is to simply be at peace with our thoughts and feelings, and to speak and act accordingly. This is what is most practical and most rewarding for us and for all those around us. We always begin right where we are, with this thought, this feeling, this speech, this action. We come back, again and again, to the moment's thought, the moment's feeling. This moment is where the presence of peace is learned, and where life is lived, and where heaven on earth is established. As we are at peace with the moment, all veils are lifted, death departs and eternity reveals Her secrets. Such secrets are what we share, with each other and the world.

I remain with you, my friend, with these simple thoughts of beauty and enrichment. Let's be at peace with each other and with the galaxies — in peace —

(Charlie)

Eleventh Letter:
Physical Healing Spontaneously Follows

Hello, Randy —

As your old friend, and in response to your gentle request, let me simply remind you of what you already know: the peaceable presence is the source, and root force of all healing, and all creation yields to its power. I have no doubt that the peace you already know is more than sufficient to meet your every need, including these current physical, as well as mental and emotional challenges. However, let me suggest that the success or failure of your ministrations of peace be not measured by any particular changes in your physical condition but rather by whether there is a resumption of peace in your inner experience. After all, to re-experience peace is why we seek changes in our physical condition. I would remind you that you are free to bypass the physical symptoms and go straight to the prize!

Nevertheless, I assure you that as you consistently begin to remember the presence of peace in your daily experience, recognizing it as your true and original identity, the physical healing which you seek will spontaneously follow. To identify not with physical harmony or disharmony, but rather with the eternal peace of present awareness itself is the "re-identification" process which transforms the world and sets all humanity free (for we are indeed one awareness). The experience of peace is immediate and physical healing can be too. Only as we cling to that which is less than peace, to the traditions and structures of our accumulated culture, are we bound to a slow recovery. Yet, paradoxically, our work is not to speed the healing but to be at peace with the moment (which speeds the healing!). As we are at peace with the thoughts we are thinking, and thus the feelings we are feeling right now, harmony radiates through our very cells.

You ask whether your current physical ailments might be divine will, whether it is a cross you are destined to carry. Let me say this clearly: No! Absolutely not. I am absolutely certain that your Father in Heaven, which is the presence of infinite peace, does *not* want you to suffer—does not expect you to carry such a cross. Is that what you want for your own children?

The suggestion that it might be divine will for us to suffer comes from mistaken tribal belief systems that evolved over centuries that were attempting to explain our earthly experiences. These belief systems, which are still with us, are cobbled together out of mostly failed, fragmented religious orthodoxies, not only from the Christian tradition but left over from primitive, pre-Christian, superstition-based animistic cultures. We can abandon such fear-based biases as soon as we see through them. Such a denial does not for an instant deny the Father's will, which is always and only for love, harmony, peace to be experienced in abundance by His children.

My understanding is that the current assumption that the Father has destined any of us to suffer is akin to the old assumption that the earth was flat and the sun revolves around it. Such assumptions at one time provided a certain mental support to physical sense impressions, but higher sense proved these assumptions erroneous. Abandoning such assumptions made way for quicker progress and wider explorations.

Let's be clear about this: the Father, which is the infinite presence of peace, has only peace in store for you, and it is from this peace that He has fashioned your destiny! You do not need to assume that your current suffering, near-death and depravation are necessary ingredients of some higher divine order. Rather, recognize that the divine order is always harmonious (how could it be divine if it were not?) and is fully operative, fully accessible right now, this instant. The signature of the dawning presence of this harmony is a spontaneous grin. You can confidently, fruitfully abandon anything that would deny this eternal presence, this infinite fact... deny anything that would deny you your grin!

Let me repeat: sickness is never a favor from God, or from the peaceable presence, nor is it punishment from God. Of course you can use this season of ill-health as an impetus to dive deeper into your exploration of the nature of consciousness. As you do so, you will discover the immutable peace, transcending time and space and form. Such a season as you are now experiencing can indeed be an impetus for spiritual growth, yet spirit—the presence of peace—is itself never the *cause* of disharmony or disease. As you recognize that God—the presence of Peace Herself—can never be the cause or creator of unhappiness or suffering, you gain the courage and strength to drop thoughts which cause you suffering. As you drop the thoughts which bring you suffering and dis-ease, your energy again begins to flow, harmony returns, and the false appearances begin to disappear.

Since sickness has no root in the presence of peace, which is the basis of your being, the quickest way to uproot sickness is by returning to this basis, remaining with your sense of the presence of peace, thought by thought, moment by moment. ("Am I at peace with this thought, yes or no?" If the answer is not an immediate and spontaneous yes, it's a no.)

Sickness is never of your own making, any more than it is of God's making. You did not create your sickness, for you are one of the Father's creators, and as such all you can ever create is beauty, harmony and peace. (I know that our physical senses would deny such meta-physical assertions. Yet isn't this a perfect season for you to drop the physical sense and rely on your metaphysical senses?) In a word: that which appears as sickness is not of your making, and thus you need not claim it.

The appearance of pain and disease and suffering are not—have never been, will never be—the result of the presence of peace. This presence has no capacity to be less than it is, which is eternal harmony, infinite happiness, wholeness. Is there a single inch in the entire universe where this infinite presence can deny or withhold its power or peace? Thus we recognize that pain, sickness and death have no reality in this eternal presence, and thus have no reality to them. They are, in the end, only "appearances," without substance, just as the appearance of water in the distance desert horizon is without substance, and has never quenched anyone's thirst.

We are divinely empowered—indeed, responsible for—claiming our total body of peace, in every instance, every moment, every circumstance. This is not difficult or strenuous. A sense of peace is our natural state of being. As we practice the presence of peace during our ordinary waking life, we more quickly return to it in times of stress and struggle. Peace is ever-available, yet is still seldom consciously employed as the harmonizing agent that it is.

To intentionally be at peace with your thoughts, many, many times a day—and to drop or re-contextualize the thoughts with which you are not at peace—is the basic healing work you can now employ. Without your own sense of peace, there is no healing, no matter how "spiritualized" thought may appear. The *mark* — the signature — of Spirit is peace, the presence of which is life and health. In the smallest details of your life — washing your hands, dressing, preparing food — and in your primary engagements with your spouse, your work, your children, your parents — in all these arenas, *be at peace* with your thoughts. From morning until night, be at peace! Your peace is your health.

The peaceable presence is always closer than even your breath. She is your un-severable companion. Do not ignore Her. She is closer to you even than this appearance of sickness. She is "deeper" in you than your symptoms. Go below the symptoms to find Her there, and wait with Her. The symptoms will have no place to rest, and will soon depart. Peace is in fact the sufficient curative agent, the unstoppable healing power. As you more and more rely on peace, She more and more fills your experience. If you are still moved to rely on medicines and manipulations, than *be at peace* with the medicines and manipulations. The healing law does not depend on whether you use or don't use these remedies. The law is peace itself, which sets you free to use or not use them!

Your deepest nature is peace, joy, love. If you are no longer at peace with the body, you will not stay with it, because it is not in your nature to do so! As you more and more identify with peace, with happiness, with love, the body conforms. On the other hand, when you identify with the body and its limitations, the transcendent *sense* of peace is often muffled (even though peace Herself is never diminished!).

174

Peace is infinitely present, and ever available. Thus you can be bold in your determination to ignore, deny, dismiss all that is unlike peace. You always begin with thought — ignoring, denying, dismissing or transforming all thoughts that cause you discomfort, irritation or suffering. When you start by "pacifying" your thoughts, you will find yourself spontaneously removing outer physical or relational conditions that likewise appear to cause you suffering. (Though in fact we *never* leave the arena of thought!)

Again, friend, let me assure you that God — spirit, truth, the universal presence — does not require pain, suffering, lack, limitation of any kind, for any reason. The sooner we deprive such appearances of their (supposedly) "divinely ordained" charade, the sooner they dissipate. Peace is the basic nature of God's universe. Let's rest in Her, regardless of what our physical senses are reporting.

You need not fight this sickness, or struggle with these appearances. Find those thoughts with which you are at peace and remain with them. Let them reveal to you more thoughts of the same kind, and other thoughts which allow your peace to grow wider and deeper in every direction. Release, as you can, concern with your body and remain involved with the process of your thoughts.

I've been practicing this for many years, so please be assured that when I take you into my thought I bring only that which I enjoy about you, with which I am at peace. Such a practice leaves no room for thinking of you in pain or discomfort. This is my way of praying for you. I see you — think of you — as a companion to

175

peace, cradled in the arms of peace, held secure in the Father-Mother's heavenly embrace. And when thoughts arise which argue against such a state—such as those thoughts surrounding unhappy symptoms or diagnoses or prognoses—if I am not at peace with such thoughts, I dismiss them, or look within them to find the peace which I know is omnipresent. Thus, I think of you only with peace.

I endeavor to follow this discipline with all the subjects of my thought. I understand this to be the very process by which heaven is revealed on earth. Let me encourage you again in this discipline. Whatever arises to your thought—be it near or far, about your own condition or someone else's—*this* becomes the arena for your work in this moment. From my own experience I can assure you that peace is indeed ever-present and more than sufficient to meet all demands, in all circumstances, even the most dire. Peace is the eternal staying power!

The proof of the presence of peace is not necessarily in the continuation of (??) your bodily form, although no law exists which would deny a physical life of 200-300-500 years or more. Rather, the proof of the presence of peace is in your immediate, momentary experience of peace—if only a grain or two more than you had in the previous moment. This "grain or two" more of peace is sufficient reason to practice these exercises.

Starting with a grain or two, the practice of the presence of peace leads to ever deeper, ever more expansive, pure and perfect experiences of peace, not only in our own lives but also in the lives of those near and far who are associated with our thought. This ever-increasing peace may or may not lead to the abandoning of your physical body, but it most surely leads to less and less reliance on your physical sense impressions. The physical body is designed as a vehicle and expression for eternal peace. The physical senses are a support of this expression, but they are neither its *cause* nor its prerequisite.

So, as you requested, this is my "prescription" for your current distress: be at peace with the thoughts you are thinking, abandon thoughts with which you are not at peace, or choose to be at peace with the thoughts that a moment before you were not at peace. Nothing else is required. You may administer this prescription hundreds of times a day. Your sense of peace is your sense of health. The peaceable presence is already there inside you. Allow yourself to sense it again and again and again.

I hold and create and magnify thoughts of you with which I am at peace. I will remain in peace with you through eternity. From here, again, we begin, old friend. .

In peace —

(*Charlie*)

Twelfth Letter:
Intelligent Awareness Pervades All Form

Hello again, Lynn—

Thank you, lady, for your lovely, lovely letter. And
such good news! What a change from last year—in
your health, your finances, your family! You confirm
my growing understanding that all healing—be it for
physical, relational or financial problems—comes about
basically by the unfolding of the presence of peace. It
would appear that you've proven again that our innate
sense of this presence of peace is indeed the universal
healing energy. Whether healing comes about through
a prescription, surgery, change of diet or manipulations
of one sort or another, the fundamental energy we are
releasing, tapping, eliciting, manipulating is always
only the energy of peace. It resides at the root of every
physical and mental, creative and curative formation or
formulae.

Here's how I understand it: peace is the base "presence" of the universe. Thus, peace is in itself perfect harmony, perfect alignment, perfect balance; the presence of peace is the source of perfect movement and growth. Moving out of sickness, poverty, lack and limitation is always a matter of moving *back into* peace, our native, primordial state. So as we attend to the presence of peace, even in its most minute expressions, then afflictions which we did not even know we had, dissolve. Those which were to come upon us are diverted. Those which racked us in the past have no more traces of their sieges. The presence of peace is both the proof and the process of heaven on earth. Your own experiences in the past year provide excellent proof of the outworking of this principle.

As you have shown, when we turn to the presence of peace we are spontaneously led to act courageously in our outer world, and simultaneously we are less troubled by the world's seeming chaos. When we attend to peace as our daily discipline we transcend our habitual identifications with the physical form and begin to identity with awareness itself. Intelligent awareness pervades all form, and yet is not limited by forms. As we release our dependence on outer forms and rest in the center-less, formless peaceable presence, our strength increases, our health improves, our pains and afflictions dissolve. I think we have discovered, and you have proven, that the habitual awareness of peace is in fact the philosopher's stone, the fountain of youth, the immortal elixir, transmuting the base material of our daily lives into golden spiritual force.

179

It seems that you have shown over this past year that the remembrance of the presence of peace — the practice of the presence of peace — is a habit that can be developed, acquired, made mature in a relatively short period of time. (A year is a relatively short period of time for such a life-changing force to be mastered!) In small and large tasks, in private and public moments, in little draughts and rushing waves, we discover and prove that peace itself is the one true and necessary companion for this life's journey. By grace, this companion has been assigned and installed into our very being, our soul, and it is through this companion that we bring this peaceable spirit into expression in our daily affairs. As you know, if we have only an inch of peace in the long yards of our lives, then it is our job to cling to and have faith in that one inch. Indeed, in some moments we feel as though we have only a half an inch, or one-fourth of an inch, one-sixteenth of an inch of peace amidst the mountain that is our life. So the work is to abandon the mountain and cling to the one-sixteenth!

Again as you have shown (it comes through in your letter!) the peaceable presence does not always make us passive or uninvolved. Led by peace, we sometimes find ourselves being quite boisterous or animated or especially full of energy and gushing positively beautiful thoughts. (And at other times it does indeed lead us to be passive and removed from the fray.) In many moments of our lives, the river of peace simply flows quietly, slowly, deeply, and everything appears quite ordinary, un-exalted. In such phases our conversation may seem unexceptional. Our tasks appear mundane. Yet we are enjoying the presence of peace in these moments as truly as in the moments when our very selves are dissolved in thunderous bliss. We are as at home in the hardware store as we are at the mountaintop.

Dear Lynn, when I think of you I think of you with deep peace. I pray you do the same for me. We can do this for each other as an affirmative method of prayer. And such prayers, for ourselves and others, do indeed heal the sick and infirm, as you have already experienced.

As you say in your letter, God does indeed reveal Himself (Herself) to us through the presence of peace. As we practice remaining with this peace—simply by thinking thoughts with which we are at peace--we more and more see God in all that we do, in everyone we meet, everywhere we go. This is why, as we rely on that one sixteenth inch of peace amidst the mountain of our lives, the mountain is moved! The Divine is at hand!

The proof of what I am saying has already been shown in your own life. From what you say, you have made the practice of peace—the practice of being at peace with your thoughts—your most important daily (and nightly!) discipline. As you have discovered, such an inner discipline brings about radical outer changes. Again, we need only a little bit, one sixteenth or less, and that's enough to begin. That small beginning is sufficient to lead us, bring us into perfect and consistent prayer, full enlightenment.

You ask about my own future plans. As you might have guessed, I've learned to let peace lead moment by moment! Peace may indeed lead me back to the east coast again next year, as you have requested. As far as traveling, it's unclear right now whether I'll be travelling alone or with companions, whether I'll keep my work private or bring it into more public purview. And candidly, lately I'm not even sure that peace intends for me to stay in this physical body much longer!

All I can say for sure is that my future holds more and more peace. I am confident of this because I've learned that my enjoyment of the presence of peace does not depend on my body, or my circumstance. It is for this reason that I remain devoted to Her. I remain happy. My life is simple in this respect.

Let me also suggest that when we take up this simple discipline, as you have done, we unknowingly take hundreds of thousands along with us. One person can not enjoy the presence of peace without opening the door for this presence to flow in new ways across the earth. As the scriptures confirm, it is the Father's good pleasure to give us His Kingdom—this continual sense of peace. In the manner and to the extent we have prepared ourselves to accept this presence, that much He gives us, and more if we were but to open to it!

So let us continue to share this singular presence of peace. (It is no secret that it is the same peaceable presence that we each access in our own time and place. There is only one presence, unlimited by time or space.) This singular "root energy" is what we have to share, our only reason for acquaintance. As we do this—share and exchange our peace—the light of the world is lit again. Harmony is restored, in our minds and bodies.

Let us discover and confirm together this basic healing practice. Without peace, we have no harmony. With peace, we spontaneously exhibit healing powers.

We can each be at peace with our thoughts and feelings in every moment, and yet peace is never depleted by our indulgence in it. Indeed, the expression of peace expands as our attention holds to it. We can profitably return our attention, time and time again, to the reservoir of peace at the base of our thought— which, indeed, surrounds and upholds our thought. We have found the key to the kingdom. Let us open the door again and again. Peace is the very air we breathe. We can safely abandon anything that arises in our thought that is unlike peace, and thus "live and move and have our being" in this invisible delight.

I hold you — perceive you — in this peaceable radiance. Please think of me with pleasure and delight. Our exchange on these terms redeems the world.

In Joy, Peace and Prosperity —

(Charlie)

Thirteenth Letter:
Trust Your Own Sense of Peace

Hello again, Randy —

I know your physical struggles continue. Please know that my heart and my prayerful support are with you in this difficult season, old friend. Yet from our talk I also recognize that you are more and more practicing the "pacification" of your thoughts. As you know, this practice is, itself, a very healthy state of being. Thus (you need not worry!) I do not feel sorry for you, but rather admire your rapid growth and illumination in this season. I have no doubt that as you mature in this practice — remembering time and again to be at peace with your thoughts, to choose thoughts with which you are at peace, drop thoughts that trouble you — as you mature in this practice you will discover your physical ailments dissolving. That's been my experience with this practice and the experience of countless others with whom I've been privileged to work.

Yet to change your physical condition is not the basic purpose for this practice. The basic purpose is to simply experience a little more peace in this particular moment. Just this is a sufficient, beautiful and practical reason for taking up this work.

As we have already discussed, I no longer believe, as the old culture would suggest, that God sends pain and sorrow to His children in order that we might learn of His Love. (How twisted He would have to be!) No, I don't believe that. And if there is such a God, I hereby firmly reject Him. We humans already bring an overabundance of pain, misery and suffering to ourselves without having a Divine Hand pitching in!

Rather, I intuit that the Divine is the presence of peace itself, and that our pains and sorrows arise from the faulty training, faulty education that our culture has perpetuated over many, many centuries that would have us ignore or suppress our sense of peace. We all suffer from this faulty training, to one degree or another, as surely as the fish suffer from toxins poured into the river. Our toxins are mental and emotional, before they are physical. And our "purifying" process is this return to peace, this moment by moment practice by which we wash our mental and emotional atmospheres with the "cleansing" force of the universe. (To be precise, the presence of peace is simply the *force* of the universe—its cleansing effect is only how we humans experience, or interpret it! For peace (Peace) itself—infinite and eternal—there is nothing needing cleansing!)

In answer to your question, no, I would have no objections or reservations if you should choose to drop all (or just a few!) of your doctors, along with all (or some) of your medications, along with any of your various technological and biological treatments — anything or anyone with which you are not at peace. Peace is the key. Anything or anyone with whom you are at peace, you can safely keep. Anything or anyone with whom you are not at peace, you can safely drop.

Yes, this may seem heretical, and "contrary to medical advice." And yet, my own experience and the experience of many others give me absolute confidence that we can trust our innate sense of the presence of peace. In every case, in every decision you can trust the promptings of the presence of peace. (Again, I know such a statement may seem blasphemous to our "professional" class, but the statement comes from direct experience over many decades.) This inner sense of the presence of peace has within it the direct guidance of your deepest self, which is directly aligned with life itself. Such alignment brings about complete mental and physical rejuvenation.

You ask whether you can rely solely on the presence of peace itself. Sure, why not, if this is where peace has led you! You've already tried relying on almost everything else, and still you suffer. Let's go straight for the prize. Of course you can still use outer remedies if you are so inclined, but such outer remedies (as you have amply demonstrated) are neither necessary nor lasting. Their place is in the momentary comfort they provide to your mental and emotional expectations, and why should we argue with such momentary comforts!

With your growing maturity in the practice of the presence of peace, you will discover that your own mental expectations for and reliance on outside remedies begins to diminish. This is apparently already happening in your case. This can be taken as a sign that these physical remedies are no longer so requisite. Again, whatever you are most at peace to do—do that! *Trust* yourself in these matters—trust your own sense of peace—even if it means going against the "best advice" of your professional advisors.

That peace itself is a healing power—that it is the basic, fundamental, all purpose healing power—has until recently been almost completely ignored by the professional healing community. Where the inner sense of peace has been recognized for its healing qualities it has often been relegated to a secondary or tertiary role in the healing process. Professionals most often assume that an increase in mental buoyancy is inspired by an improvement in physical condition. The patient himself is often under this impression. If we would more closely examine these cases, however, we discover that it is a rise in the buoyancy of thought—even if only for a moment— that almost always *preceded* the turn in physical condition. I'm convinced that even those who are unconscious—and are "brought back" by physical manipulations of those in attendance—have in their inner life first found something with which they were at peace before the outer manipulations were successful. And when alert it is often the hope of the

187

curative powers of the next new medicine that in fact elicits the powers from these drugs.

Of course, from the highest perspective, the universe itself is only thought, or awareness, and what we consider to be physical, or material, is not in essence dissimilar to what we consider to be mental or spiritual. Thus, "feeling better" physically is in truth *always* a *mental* improvement. Quantum physicists are now proving this beyond doubt.

So yes, I would agree with you that some of your physical struggles might have been exacerbated by the well-meaning physicians in your attendance. In accordance with their training, they have focused almost all of their attention on the rising and falling of your physical temperatures, pressures, blood counts, etc., to the exclusion of, or with the effect of downplaying your own inner mood at the time of their examinations. Indeed, their newest analyses and diagnoses only added to and gave emphasis to those accumulated thoughts with which you have not been at peace. The quickest way now for your own healing is to forgive them. "They know not what they do."

My own focus is generally just the opposite of the medical focus. I would suggest that your physical appearance and inner aberrations are of relatively small significance in comparison to your progress—your power—in entertaining only those thoughts you enjoy, with which you are at peace and dismissing those that trouble you. This, from my experience, much more accurately charts the "progress" (decline) of your ailments! I'll say it again: the presence of peace *is* the healing force—the balancing, harmonizing, adjusting and eliminating force—which you already have "built-in" to your system to perfectly minister to your daily affairs.

So what can you do from here?

This: *Be at peace* with all of your doctors' concerns, predictions and projections, based on their love of their medical science and their concern for your recovery. They too need all the love, all the peace you can bring to them. Through your peaceable-ness with their ministrations (and perhaps your peaceable-ness in declining their ministrations), you heal not only yourself, but the whole medical profession.

And then, if you are not at peace with their particular predictions and analyses, you are free to simply dismiss them! I know this suggestion sounds dangerously heretical in our culture, where medical professionals are assumed to have final authority and we, their obeisant subjects, must accept whatever thoughts and analyses and projections they give us! Nevertheless, I stick with my claim: the most practical thing you can do for yourself and those around you is to remember peace in every relationship and every circumstance. Thus, it is most practical to dismiss all troubling analyses, all unhappy predictions, because you are divinely entitled to claim your place, right now, in the perfect harmony here unfolding! (Again, I recognize that in terms of traditional healing orthodoxy, this advice is heretical stuff. But it is *stuff* the efficiency of which I have seen proven time and time again!)

189

Whether you accept your doctors' analyses or dismiss them, the intent is always and only and specifically to restore your sense of peace, (or more accurately, to restore your *remembrance*, your awareness of the presence of peace, for in fact peace has never left!). If the thought of dismissing your doctors' advice leaves you very troubled, then don't dismiss it. If such thought brings you back to peace, you're on safe ground.

Here's the healing principle: Whatever aids you in this restoration—remembrance—of the presence of peace is beneficial. Whatever delays, or dampens, or downplays your sense of peace can be confidently abandoned! Peace is the key. Have I said it clearly and boldly enough?

I would recommend to you the contemplation of the presence of peace as the "first energy" of the universe, or peace as the "essence" of all energy now extant. Consider the possibility that peace is the essence of solar energy and of wind energy and of all the mechanical-electrical energy we use; Peace is the essence of our bodily energy, from the DNA intelligence to the molecular attraction and denial, to the beating of the heart and the inflow and out-flow of the breath. As you spend time contemplating the *allness* of peace—the omnipresence of peace—even if only on a theoretical basis, you'll soon discover that even the birds will sing out to confirm your speculations. The contemplation of peace—thinking about it, wondering, speculating, postulating—is a way of spending time with peace. And this is what is most needed, not only when we are physically challenged, but *always*.

190

Contemplating peace (Peace) will lead you to the right use of your physical energies. Contemplating peace will help you to conserve energy when you need to conserve it and spend it when you need to spend it. Contemplating the nature of peace—both within and without the physical body—brings balance into your life. Attending first to the presence of peace, you'll discover that you more often do what you need to do exactly when you need to do it and you cease doing what is no longer necessary or beneficial. Such actions are in fact fairly spontaneous, arising naturally out of your awareness of the presence of peace.

I'll say it again, quite simply: allowing yourself to be at peace in every relationship and in every circumstance is the basic foundation for deep healing. You allow yourself to be at peace simply by being at peace with your thoughts, and releasing thoughts with which you are not at peace. So simple, so powerful a tool!

Do not wait for peace until *after* your healing is accomplished. Rather, seek it right here, in the midst of struggles. Begin now, to whatever degree you have trained yourself, to be at peace with your thoughts, even if you can only find a single thought with which to be at peace. And when you have found such a thought, stick with it until another thought arises which reveals a little more peace than the previous one. And then watch for the next thought, and the next one. Be at peace with your thoughts one after another, and if you find yourself forgetting your peace, the best solution is to be at peace with your forgetfulness! (And at peace with your eventual remembering.)

191

This is, as you see, a very simple discipline. Very direct. Very "hands on" in the sense that we always begin right where we are, with the thoughts we are thinking this instant. What could be simpler?

You do not need to melt the doors off the barn with your practice of peace, though some moments, some days may indeed seem to dissolve everything into peaceable radiance. To be at peace in simple, ordinary ways is quite appropriate. Peace contains all hues, all colors, all tones, all the highs and lows. Peace is ever-present in every moment and we can profitably abandon all that is unlike Her and cling to the slightest indication of Her Presence. For even Her slightest indication is more real and more powerful than all the galaxies of suffering!

We need not search for the end of suffering but rather for the beginning—the re-beginning, re-emergence—of peace. Time and time again—with thought after thought—we search for the re-emergence of the presence of peace and time and again we are not disappointed. This is the building of the New Heaven and the New Earth. This is the work which reveals the eternal presence.

I realize that what I am suggesting here—that you re-discover your own sense of peace, if only one thought at a time, amidst the physical suffering you experience—is contrary to what your attention might at first find compelling. Your attention naturally drifts to your pains, your discomfort, the doctors' predictions and all that which seems to be at the root of your suffering. And yet, as you place your attention again and again onto those things, people, events, possibilities, ideas, prayers and meditations with which you are peace, you are nourished and upheld by that very force which is prior to and the remedy for your distress. Placing your attention on the presence of peace — in whatever form appears to you in this moment — gives energy and strength and provides a certain distance from suffering. To let your difficulties be a prompting towards this training is to use them in their highest potential.

That you might train yourself to return your thoughts again and again to what you enjoy does not require the presence of pain and discomfort and yet such presence does provide constant impetus for such training. This process of returning your attention to peace and happiness again and again is the equivalent of learning to pray without ceasing.

In fact, the basic reason we all wish to be free of our pains — be our pains large or small — is simply so that we might be at peace again, enjoy ourselves again. So again, I encourage you to not wait until your pains have subsided. You are divinely designed to be at peace unconditionally in all times and places and circumstances. Nothing in this universe has been granted power to remove you from the presence of peace. You alone, bestow such an endarkening right. Deny such claims; return to your inheritance!

Peace is present, old friend. That is our refuge. Peace is present, even closer than the air we breathe, the light by which we see, the earth on which we stand. Peace is present. This is our saving truth. We are designed to turn to peace, rely on peace, companion with peace, in every moment. We are the children of peace. She has not abandoned us, nor can She ever abandon us.

I'm a stuck record: *Return to your peace — be at peace with your thoughts, one by one, moment after moment —* and see if your day is not filled with Grace. I wait with you, live with you, move with you in this Presence, and recognize you as completely embraced by this shared, peaceable destiny. There is no possibility that it could be any other way. And I joyfully recognize your own recognition of this Grace.

My own peace is here when I think of you with these thoughts. I'll write again, soon, and think of you often.

In peace —

(*Charlie*)

Fourteenth Letter:
Peace Is Willing and Ready to Play

Hello again, Lynn—

I of course share your happiness, and am deeply pleased to hear that your physical condition continues to be completely normal. As your doctors said (though not in these words), it was clear that a year ago you were close to the point of dropping your physical body. It was just as clear, however, at least to us, that your peace did in fact remain with you. You have witnessed, and demonstrated for us all, both the power and the faithfulness of the presence of peace. I happily receive your expression of gratitude toward me, and I return it to you a hundred-fold: thank *you* for the beautiful work you have done and the demonstration you have made.

Since She (Peace) did not abandon you during these difficult hours, you can easily recognize how willing and ready She is to play with you in your ordinary days amidst your ordinary tasks and pastimes. So you can simply continue to be as faithful to Her, my friend, as She is to you. As you know, She is quite deserving of every devotion, every consideration, every thought, feeling and action you might dedicate to Her. Her companionship is both the proof and the path of heaven on earth.

The presence of peace, though eternal, infinite, omnipotent and omnipresent, is, for our special human convenience, also present as the small comforting fire lit in our hearts which warms our hands, our feet and our heads. As our thoughts flow through, we learn to gently bend them toward Her flames. Those that will not bend, we gently abandon. To be at peace with all of our thoughts, all day long, is how we companion with peace, companion with God. As we do so, the flame grows brighter. This, you have already experienced.

In answer to your question, yes, I suspect it is possible to be at peace with every thought, even the most forbidden and corrupt. It is not the *content* of the thought that we are experiencing or affirming, but rather the peace that is, in essence, formless, timeless, spaceless, (thus thoughtless!). Nevertheless, there are thoughts with which we are not at peace and have no interest in trying to be at peace with them, just for the sake of demonstration. So when we are not immediately at peace with a particular thought, we are free to simply dismiss it for later attention. (Anything we are not at peace with is automatically returned to the storehouse and may be presented again later.)

I am now convinced that the *only* purpose of our thoughts arising is so that we might explore more variations of the presence of peace. (The only purpose of the arising of the universe is so that we might explore the presence of peace!) Thoughts that arise with which we are not at peace therefore do not fulfill their purpose, their function. (And that is why they will, sooner or later, return again that their purposes might be fulfilled!)

It is a sacred flame—this peace—that is burning in our hearts. In our Christian tradition it is known as the Holy Spirit, or the Christ Consciousness. In other traditions this same flame is known as Allah, or Brahma or *atman* or Emmanuel or *satchitananda*, the Buddha mind, the Deep Mind, the Pure Land, the Tao, the Te, Wakanda...the names for this presence are countless. Still, in every tradition, Its signature is always: peace.

As you allow your thoughts to be engulfed, and consumed by this peaceable flame, your very presence reveals itself as a Holy Site, a temple of the living God. As you remain with peace, you remain with the temple, and thus does your physical body gently come into alignment with the harmony which animates your thinking stream (and the universe itself!). Nevertheless, as you have so wonderfully demonstrated, regardless what your physical body is registering in any particular moment of time and space, you are ever empowered to remain in, abide in the temple of peace. This is our inheritance!

As we practice being at peace with our thoughts, even as beginners, we immediately experience the fruits of the practice. (I have been practicing for fifty years now, and I often still feel like a beginner!) This is not a practice which we take up with the hope of eventual reward. This practice itself — choosing thoughts with which we are peace and choosing to be at peace with thoughts that arise — is rewarding, enriching, enlightening, from its first engagement. Our continuing practice confirms and strengthens and deepens our peace, and Peace Itself moves in our lives to authenticate and sanctify our experience. Peace is infinite, and thus there is no room we can occupy, no space on earth or off of earth where peace is not. And peace is eternal, so that there is no time, now, or in the past, or in the future, where we are forbidden or denied access to the presence of peace.

Our momentary individual awareness of peace leads us into understanding and acceptance and delight in the infinite and eternal presence of peace which is our lawful and unbreakable inheritance. There is nothing in the universe which has the power to keep us from this inheritance, from accepting it, experiencing it, either sooner or later. We are learning together to allow this peace to come sooner — here, now — in our own humble lives, that through our lives the whole world might be blessed.

And let us admit that the world *is* blessed, right now, by these letters we share, expressing the peaceable presence by which we are already bonded. Even if these physical letters are never shared with another soul, still, peace is released in both of us as we share them and the measure of peace in the world is higher for it. What joy to be here, in ordinary time and space, and simultaneously abiding in that timeless, spaceless presence aflame in our hearts.

Mother-Father-God, Abba-Allah-Amma, Joy, Bliss, Peace, we are yours, unconditionally, all through this experience here on this earth. Through our attention to peace, present in our simple, ordinary awareness, our shackles fall away, and the light is again delightfully revealed.

In great friendship and awakening —

I am yours —

(Charlie)

Fifteenth Letter:
This Is the Sentient Physics of the Universe

Hello once again, Linda,

Your questions always bring out the best in me. Thank you!

To answer your question, my understanding now, in Christian terms, is that Christ never withholds His Peace from us. It is His pleasure to give us His Peaceable Kingdom. And so He does, continually, uninterruptedly. This is the work the Father has given Him to do.

Thus, the amount of peace we experience in our lives depends almost completely on our training, and our willingness to accept, to receive the treasures ever pouring forth from His fount. We are *never* denied the comfort of peace or its healing power. This peace that is already residing within us is always sufficient to meet our every circumstance, if only we would avail ourselves of it. This is the sentient physics of the universe.

The presence of peace is forever undiminished, unblemished. She never sends, or supports, or sanctifies *any* unhappiness, or disharmony or discord. That which would appear as suffering is dissolved as we turn again to Her Grace, Her gifts. We need not hold to anything but peace. (As you know, the Divine can not be described with the words He, She, It, Christ, and yet these words each reflect a particular character of the Divine. I find myself now freely using them all, interchangeably, as my sense of the Divine has expanded to reveal such wonders!)

We are *lawfully* entitled — indeed, commanded — to dispense with all that is unlike Peace (the Divine). All thoughts, theories, opinions, judgments, analyses, decisions or symptoms which do not express the peaceable presence do not reflect the underlying reality and thus can be safely, and fruitfully, abandoned. The peaceable presence is centermost in our being not because we have *decided* to put it there, but because it was there *before* we were formed out of its Presence, its Substance. Peace is our own original nature. We need not struggle in pursuit of it any more than we need to struggle in pursuit of our eye color. The closer we come to the presence of peace, the closer we come to ourselves.

Intelligence and peace are two more words describing the same essence, the same Creative Presence. We come to understand and experience peace not only through our emotions, but also through our intellect. As we focus on peace, which might be described as the central sun of all creation, as we focus of that presence, duality dissolves and the peaceable oneness of the creation appears. In this oneness, (Oneness), there is no fear of duality, nor struggle with sense appearances. Both pleasure and pain are resolved in and by grace.

Practicing the presence of peace—holding to thoughts with which we are at peace—is not a means to an end. Practicing peace is itself the culmination of all human striving. By practicing peace we may indeed find ourselves removed from poverty, blessed with a nurturing family and friends, drawn into deeper intimacy with our spouse, propelled on profitable adventures both near and far. And yet, to gain such material manifestations, such relationships and circumstances is not the intent of our moment by moment practice. Such positive unfoldings in our lives are but the natural and spontaneous residue of attending to peace. Peace itself remains with us throughout eternity. All else arises and fades away.

Our peace is an inner stream from which we might construct first a pond, then a lake, then a reservoir by which we provide nourishment to the world. The depth and the breadth of our peace grow according to our willingness to abandon our demands for satisfaction from without, drawing instead from the life reservoir within. At last, we are engulfed in the ocean.

On this path, we naturally enjoy the daily experience of friends, food, nature's beauty and our various social unfoldments. And yet, less and less does our awareness of peace depend on any of these, as we mature more and more in the practices here set forth.

Let me again say it clearly, simply: The inner discipline of peace — of attending to thoughts with which we are at peace, dropping thoughts which cause turmoil or divisiveness — is the highest, most natural and most fruitful of all disciplines. When we make this our primary daily discipline, then over a lifetime we steadily grow more adept at experiencing the presence of peace in absolutely every single thought, and thus in all our relations, all our activities, all our work and leisure hours. This discipline includes taking the time to "clean" those thoughts with which we are not at peace, that we might abide solely with what is pleasant and true. Peace Herself aids us in this discipline. One step in Her direction elicits ten from Her in our direction. And soon we see that in truth the distance between us was all along illusory.

We share with each other this peace. Your recent recovery was not the proof of Her return but rather the evidence of Her continued abiding. I sense for myself an imminent release from these comings and goings, that I might abide with Her uninterruptedly.[2] But this is how it has been for many years.

Let us enjoy and be at peace with each other, in whatever way we can, today. Tomorrow we will enjoy each other, and this world, in ways different from what we now know. Yet, we will be ready — our practice, and Peace Herself, prepares the way.

I remain, in peace, always yours —

(Charlie)

---

[2] Two days after this letter was written, Dr. Charlie died peaceably in his sleep.

About the Author

Bear Jack Gebhardt, senior librarian at Heart Mountain Monastery (www.heartmountainmonastery.net) practices peace and bonsai cultivation from his home in the foothills of the Rockies in northern Colorado. He is the author of numerous books, both fiction and non-fiction, and is a popular speaker and presenter with spiritual and professional communities here and abroad. He lives with his wife, Suzanne and Rocky, their toy poodle. They have two grown children. Bear can be contacted at bear@heartmountainmonastery.net

About the Cover Designer

Sam Gebhardt (www.samgebhardt.com) is an artist living and working in Los Angeles CA, with his wife Angela and two dogs, Daisy and Suzy. Sam works in the video-game and film industries. He has credits on films such as *The Aviator, Shrek 2* and *Open Season*, to name a few.

Order More Copies of
Practicing the Presence of Peace

Price:
$18.95 + 3.95 Shipping
5+ Copies: $14.50 each + Free Domestic Shipping!
10+ Copies: $13.25 + Free Domestic Shipping for up to 20 copies

Number of Copies: _____ $_____.____
Shipping: $_____.____
Total: $_____.____

Ship to:
    Name_____

    Address_____

    City_____ State_____

            Zip Code_____

Mail Checks to:
PathBinder Publishing, LLC
1701 Banyan Ct
Charlottesville, VA 22911

For Visa/Master Card orders, call 434-466-4338

Questions? E-mail Heather@PathBinder.com
    Or call 434-466-4338

205

Practicing the Presence of Peace